D1492570

POCKET REFERENCE GUIDES

WEATHER

A guide to recognizing different weather
phenomena and understanding their causes.
Illustrated throughout in colour

Eleanor Lawrence & Borin van Loon

BROCKHAMPTON PRESS

The author and publisher acknowledge the help given by **The Met. Office**, Bracknell, who kindly gave their permission to use information from their publications in the compilation of the weather maps on pages 27 and 119–121.

Front cover illustration: Cumulonimbus clouds

This edition published in 2000 by
Brockhampton Press,
20 Bloomsbury Street,
London WC1B 3QA,

This edition produced under licence by
Malcolm Saunders Publishing Ltd, London

A CIP Catalogue record for this book is available from the British Library

Title: Pocket Reference Guides, WEATHER
ISBN: 1 86019 779 5

Printed in China by Colorcraft

Contents

INTRODUCTION — 8

HOW TO USE THIS BOOK — 8

WHAT IS WEATHER? — 11

GLOSSARY — 12

THE ATMOSPHERE — 14

WEATHER SYSTEMS — 26

CLOUDS — 37

PRECIPITATION: Rain, Snow & Hail — 68

WINDS — 82

OPTICAL & ATMOSPHERIC PHENOMENA — 93

CLIMATE — 102

OBSERVATION & FORECASTING — 112

INDEX — 122

Introduction

The weather affects us all, but we rarely stop to consider its causes until extreme weather conditions put people to inconvenience or in danger. Hurricanes, floods and droughts hit the headlines as they bring tragedy to thousands of people. They are a reminder of the power of the forces that generate the weather, which most of us thankfully experience in a less dreadful guise. The weather is the one thing we cannot control. The best we can do is to study it carefully so that we can be forewarned about what it will bring.

Following the day-to-day changes in the weather and getting to know your local conditions can be a fascinating and rewarding pastime. This book helps you recognize different types of weather and weather phenomena and explains how they are caused. It will help you get started on keeping a record of the weather, and as your knowledge increases you will be able to recognize for yourself the local signs that the weather is changing for better or worse.

How to use this book

The book is divided into eight sections: **The Atmosphere**; **Weather Systems**; **Clouds**; **Precipitation (Rain, Snow and Hail)**; **Winds**; **Optical and Atmospheric Phenomena**; **Climate** and **Observation and Forecasting**. Each section is indicated by a different colour band at the top of each page together with an identification symbol. In the section on **The Atmosphere** some basic information is given to help you understand how weather is produced; in **Weather Systems**, the main types of weather systems and their associated weather are illustrated and explained; the section on **Clouds** explains how clouds are formed and illustrates many of the different types; in **Precipitation** we explain how rain, hail and snow are produced; the section on **Winds** deals with winds and phenomena such as hurricanes that generate strong winds; the section on **Optical and Atmospheric Phenomena** illustrates some of the wonderful sights you can see in the sky; a selection of world climates are defined in the section on **Climates**; and the final section on **Observation and Forecasting** provides advice on making your own weather observations. Several sections also include weather conditions and types of pollution relevant to the main section topic.

The Atmosphere

This section provides some background information on the atmosphere and the properties of air that are necessary to understand how weather is formed. Also included here are pages on the 'greenhouse effect' and on the 'holes' in the ozone layer.

Weather Systems

This section deals with the main larger-scale influences on our weather, including air masses, fronts, and high- and low-pressure systems, and shows how they are depicted on a weather map.

Clouds

Here you will find descriptions and illustrations of the main types of clouds and how they are formed. Also included are some special clouds that occur in particular situations. Fog, dew and frost are also covered here as their formation is very similar to that of clouds, except that they are produced at ground level.

Precipitation (Rain, Hail and Snow)

This section includes a description of the water cycle and illustrates how rain, hail and snow are produced, and some of the weather conditions associated with them.

Winds

In this section the nature and classification of winds are described as well as some local winds and weather phenomena with which winds are associated, such as hurricanes, tornadoes and waterspouts.

Optical and Atmospheric Phenomena

This section describes and illustrates how light causes optical phenomena like rainbows, haloes and coronas. It also covers thunderstorms, lightning, and the aurora.

Climate

This section gives a map of world climates and describes individually eight different types.

Observation and Forecasting

This section explains how weather forecasts are produced and some of the instruments you need to make your own weather observations. Examples of weather maps show how the basic information gathered is used in different ways — to make a detailed chart from which an official forecast will be produced; to help you plan your holiday destination; and to provide ships at sea with up-to-date weather bulletins.

Now you are ready to use this book. If you wish, you can study the weather in your own local area from the comfort of an armchair in front of the window. But take a trip out from time to time, especially in changeable weather, to where you can see the whole sweep of the sky. And remember to take this book with you on outings to places where the weather is different from that at home — to the coast, perhaps, or the mountains. Have a fine day!

Specimen page

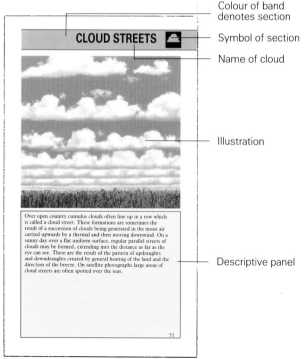

Colour of band denotes section

Symbol of section

Name of cloud

Illustration

Descriptive panel

CLOUD STREETS

Over open country cumulus clouds often line up in a row which is called a cloud street. These formations are sometimes the result of a succession of clouds being generated in the moist air carried upwards by a thermal and then moving downwind. On a sunny day over a flat uniform surface, regular parallel streets of clouds may be formed, extending into the distance as far as the eye can see. These are the result of the pattern of updraughts and downdraughts created by general heating of the land and the direction of the breeze. On satellite photographs large areas of cloud streets are often spotted over the seas.

51

What is Weather?

Our weather is the outcome of the unique combination of the type of atmosphere our planet possesses, its abundant water, and our distance from the Sun. A little nearer, and we might be permanently shrouded in stifling cloud; farther away, water would be permanently frozen.

The powerful force driving the weather is ultimately the Sun's energy. This sets the air in the atmosphere moving and solar energy is also stored and released when water is converted from liquid to vapour to ice and back again. As the air responds to changes in temperature by becoming lighter or heavier, wetter or drier, clouds are formed, rain falls, air pressure changes and winds blow.

The weather we experience at any particular place and time is the result of the prevailing conditions in the layer of the atmosphere nearest the surface. All our weather is generated in the troposphere, this densest and lowest part of the atmosphere. Conditions here vary from hour to hour throughout the day, from day to day, from place to place and from season to season as the Earth, tilted on its axis, makes its annual journey around the Sun. Different parts of the Earth experience different patterns of weather throughout the year, and this is their climate.

For everyday purposes we usually only need to describe the weather as fine, fair, bad or foul. Meteorologists, however, must record and describe prevailing weather conditions more precisely, in terms of a combination of temperature, air pressure, humidity, cloud type and cover, visibility, precipitation, and wind speed and direction. The atmosphere is such a complicated physical machine that in most places, the weather it will generate on any particular day in the future is still almost completely unpredictable for more than a few days ahead. Using the knowledge gathered from over a hundred years of detailed weather observations, from satellite observations and from powerful computer models of atmospheric behaviour, short-term weather forecasts are now usually very accurate. But whether the day of the summer fête planned long in advance will be warm and sunny or cold and rainy is still very much a matter of chance, and is something we cannot control.

Glossary

adiabatic refers to warming and cooling of air by the effects of expansion and compression under the influence of pressure alone, without any external sources of heating or cooling.

altitude height above sea level.

condensation conversion of water vapour into liquid water.

condensation point the temperature at which water starts to condense out of air. It varies with humidity of the air.

continental refers to lands away from the oceans and whose climates are not subject to their moderating influence.

convection the vertical movement of air or water as a result of temperature changes.

dew point see **condensation point**.

diffraction the bending of light around obstacles such as air molecules and water droplets.

evaporation the conversion of water from liquid to vapour.

inversion a layer of cool air trapped by warmer air above it.

isobars lines on weather chart joining points of equal surface pressure.

lee, leeward the side of a mountain range or other obstruction facing away from the prevailing wind.

maritime refers to countries bordering the oceans and whose climates are influenced by the moderating effect of the ocean.

meteorology the study of the weather and the atmosphere.

mid-latitudes latitudes between around 30 and 70° N or S.

precipitation rain, snow or hail.

refraction the bending of light as it passes from one transparent medium, e.g. air, into another of different density, e.g. water.

saturated refers to air holding the maximum amount of water vapour it can at that temperature, i.e. it has a relative humidity of 100%. The **saturation point** of air is the temperature at which it becomes saturated.

stable refers to air in which there is little vertical movement. If air is forced to rise in a stable environment it will soon become cooler than its surroundings and will sink back towards the surface. Stability depends in complex ways on temperature and humidity; as a general rule air that is cool near the surface and warmer higher up is generally stable. See also **unstable**.

stratosphere the layer of the atmosphere immediately above the troposphere.

supercooled refers to water droplets that have cooled to below freezing point but do not freeze because of their small size.

tropical lying between latitudes 23° 27′ N (Tropic of Cancer) and 23° 27′ S (Tropic of Capricorn), between which the Sun is directly overhead at some time of the year.

tropopause the boundary between troposphere and stratosphere.

troposphere the lowest and densest layer of the atmosphere in which our weather occurs.

turbulence irregularities in wind speed and direction.

unstable refers to air in which there is a tendency for vertical movement. If air is forced to rise in an unstable environment it will soon become or remain warmer than its surroundings and continue to rise. Instability depends in complex ways on temperature and humidity; as a general rule air that is warm near the surface and much colder higher up is generally unstable. See also **stable**.

Symbols used on weather maps

Weather

〵 Drizzle	= Mist		
• Rain	∞ Haze		
✳ Snow	⌢ Smoke haze		
△ Hail	≡ Fog		
▽ Showers	≡≡ Fog patches		
⪽ Thunderstorm			
⋎ Squall			
⪦ Thundery showers			

Cloud types

⌐⌐	Cirrus
≤	Cirrostratus
⌇	Cirrocumulus
⪤	Altostratus
⌣	Altocumulus
⊐⊔	Stratocumulus
—	Stratus
⪥	Nimbostratus
⌂	Cumulus
⌂	Cumulonimbus

Wind speed

◎ Calm		⦌⦌⦌ 30 knots	
⟋— 5 knots		⦌⦌⦌ 35 knots	
⟍— 10 knots		⦌⦌⦌ 45 knots	
⟍ 15 knots		◣— 50 knots	
⟍ 20 knots		◣— 60 knots	
⟍ 25 knots		◣⦌ 70 knots	

Cloud cover

●	Overcast
◕	⅞ sky covered
◕	6/8
◑	5/8
◐	½
◑	3/8
◔	¼
◔	⅛
○	Clear sky

Fronts

▲▲	Cold front
●●	Warm front
▲●▲●	Occluded front

The Atmosphere

The atmosphere envelops the Earth in a protective blanket of gases, extending several thousand kilometres out into space. This envelope is densest at the Earth's surface, rapidly thinning out with height. Without an atmosphere the Earth would be subject to the extremes of temperature experienced by the airless Moon; there would be no weather, and there would be no life. The atmosphere is divided into several distinct layers with different temperature gradients, compositions and properties. Most of our weather is formed in the lowest layer, the troposphere, which contains 90% of all the temperature by mass. This is the layer influenced by the atmosphere and topography of the Earth's surface. The air in the troposphere is constantly in motion, stirred and mixed by the transfer of heat from the sun-warmed Earth. The **temperature**, **pressure** and **humidity** of air in the troposphere is continually changing and it is these changes that make our weather.

A thin boundary layer — the tropopause — divides the troposphere from the stratosphere and marks the furthest extent of the Earth's influence on atmospheric temperature. Air temperature decreases with altitude up to the tropopause where it stops decreasing. The tropopause forms a ceiling on our weather and the stratosphere above is free of cloud and relatively calm. Aeroplanes often fly at or just above the tropopause to avoid cloud and turbulence. The height of the tropopause above the surface varies from around 10 km at the poles to 17 km over the tropics. Within the stratosphere lies the **ozone layer**. This absorbs much of the ultraviolet radiation from the Sun, shielding the Earth's surface from its harmful effects.

Composition of the air

Air in the troposphere consists mainly of nitrogen (76%) and oxygen (21%), with small amounts of carbon dioxide (around 0.03%), water vapour (1–4%), argon and hydrogen. As far as weather is concerned, the most important ingredient is water vapour. This evaporates into the air from the Earth's surface, condenses into **clouds** and is returned to the Earth as **rain** and **snow**. Air also contains minute particles of dust and salt; these provide surfaces on which water droplets condense. The air now also contains chemical pollutants, many of which are formed as we burn fossil fuels in our homes, factories and cars. These contribute to the haze and **smog** above cities.

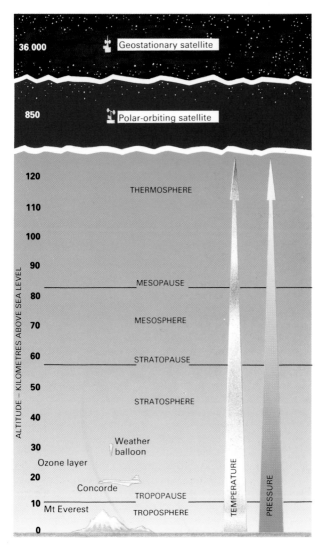

36 000   Geostationary satellite

850   Polar-orbiting satellite

ALTITUDE – KILOMETRES ABOVE SEA LEVEL

120

THERMOSPHERE

110

100

90

MESOPAUSE

80

70   MESOSPHERE

60   STRATOPAUSE

50

STRATOSPHERE

40

30   Weather balloon

Ozone layer

20

Concorde

TROPOPAUSE

10   Mt Everest   TROPOSPHERE

0

TEMPERATURE   PRESSURE

Ozone concentration in stratosphere

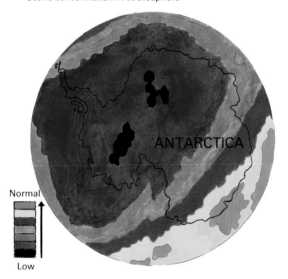

In the stratosphere there is a layer of ozone molecules (O_3) which is thickest between 15 and 25 km above the Earth's surface. Ozone is continually being formed from oxygen (O_2) by the action of sunlight and decays slowly back into oxygen. The ozone layer blankets out most of the Sun's ultraviolet rays, protecting life on Earth from the harmful effects of this radiation. Ultraviolet radiation causes mutations; even with the low levels reaching us now, excessive exposure to sun can cause skin cancers, especially in light-skinned people. Some years ago, scientists found that the ozone layer had thinned by as much as a half in places. These 'holes' in the layer appear above the Antarctic in October (illustration) and the Arctic in spring. At the same time it was found that chlorofluorocarbons (CFCs), chemicals that were commonly used as propellants in aerosols and as refrigerants, were powerful destroyers of ozone and might be contributing to the thinning of the layer. Light acts on CFCs to release chlorine, which in turn reacts with ozone, splitting it into oxygen and ClO. The manufacture and use of CFCs is now decreasing.

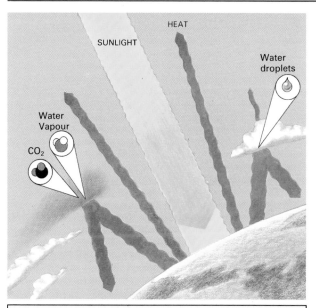

As you go further away from the Earth's surface the air in the troposphere gets colder. This is because air in this layer of the **atmosphere** is not warmed directly by the Sun, but by contact with the surface of the Earth. The outermost layers of the atmosphere are intensely hot, as they absorb X-rays and other very short wavelengths from the solar radiation. But most solar radiation that reaches the Earth's surface is in the visible light wavelengths, which pass through air without being absorbed. Light is absorbed by the surface, which warms up and emits radiation as heat (the infra-red wavelengths). This warms the air above the surface as the molecules of water vapour (H_2O) and carbon dioxide (CO_2) in air absorb radiation in these wavelengths. They also re-radiate energy as heat. If all the heat radiated by the Earth were lost upwards into space the Earth would be a much colder place. But most heat is directed back towards the Earth's surface from the bases of clouds and from the air itself — the **greenhouse effect** — so that the overall heat budget is balanced. The average temperature at the surface is 15 °C, but temperature varies enormously from place to place.

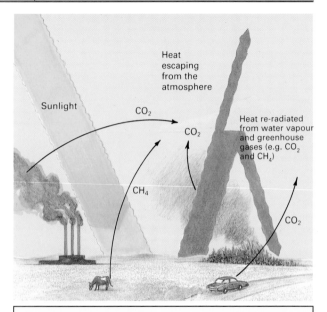

Sunlight

CO_2

CH_4

CO_2

Heat escaping from the atmosphere

Heat re-radiated from water vapour and greenhouse gases (e.g. CO_2 and CH_4)

CO_2

The **atmosphere** allows visible light through, but water vapour, carbon dioxide (CO_2) and some other natural and man-made gases in the atmosphere (the 'greenhouse gases') absorb much of the heat emitted by the Earth and re-radiate it back to the surface. This is popularly known as the greenhouse effect, and is important in regulating the Earth's temperature. The amount of carbon dioxide in the atmosphere is small (0.03%), but has been rising steadily over the past century as the result of massive burning of fossil fuels (gas, oil and coal) in the industrial world. This puts more carbon dioxide into the atmosphere than is currently being removed by photosynthesis into long-term storage in forests. Since 1958, for example, atmospheric CO_2 has increased by 11%. Many scientists now believe that an unchecked increase in CO_2 and other greenhouse gases could contribute to a serious rise in the Earth's surface temperature in the future. It is estimated that a doubling of atmospheric CO_2 could lead to a rise of between 1.5 and 5.5 °C. Such warming could change climates drastically and might even melt polar ice, raising sea level around the world and threatening many centres of population.

ATMOSPHERIC PRESSURE

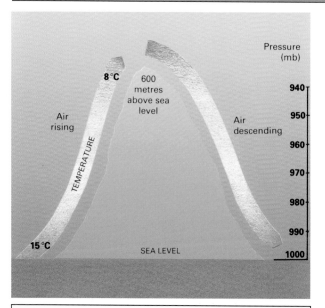

Pressure (mb)

940
950
960
970
980
990
1000

8 °C

600 metres above sea level

Air rising

Air descending

TEMPERATURE

15 °C

SEA LEVEL

The mass of the **atmosphere** exerts pressure, averaging 1013 millibars (mb) at the Earth's surface. Pressure at sea level may rise or fall by up to 50 mb in a day, but we do not sense changes in pressure unless they occur very suddenly, as the pressure of air within our bodies rapidly equalizes to that outside. Air pressure decreases with height above the Earth as the atmosphere gets thinner. Near the surface, for the first 1000 metres or so, pressure falls at a rate of approximately 1 mb per 10 metres altitude and at a height of around 5.5 kilometres pressure averages 500 mb, half that at the surface. Horizontal differences in air pressure generate winds, as air flows from an area of high pressure into a low pressure area. The vertical decrease in pressure has very important effects on the properties of the air. Air that is forced to rise for any reason expands as the pressure exerted on it becomes less. Expanding air cools down. Conversely, sinking air becomes compressed. Compressed air warms up. The warming and cooling of air by changes in pressure alone are known as adiabatic warming and cooling and are important in many weather phenomena.

The General Circulation

The large-scale circulation of air in the troposphere is caused by the unequal heating of the surface of the globe. Temperature differences between the Equator and poles and between land and sea generate the great air movements that provide the framework for all our weather. Within latitudes 35° North and South, the Earth's surface receives more radiation than it loses as heat, but at the poles it receives less than it loses (see diagram below). If heat were not continually transported polewards from the Equator, tropical regions would become hotter and polar regions colder. The atmosphere is one agent of this heat transfer; the other is the ocean. The global atmospheric circulation is extraordinarily complex and scientists do not yet understand it completely. (See p. 21.)

The general circulation produces the strong dependable winds that blow across the open oceans, such as the Trade Winds in the tropics and the prevailing westerlies further north and south (see **Global Winds**). At the Equator itself, the rising air creates the windless doldrums. The general flow of air eastwards across the Pacific and the northern Atlantic means that much of our weather moves in from the west, especially when it can travel uninterrupted over the wide reaches of the ocean. Winter storms brewed over the North Atlantic are driven eastwards to lash the western and northern coasts of Europe, and in summer settled fine weather is often the result of a large area of high pressure drifting in from warm Atlantic waters. The general eastward trend of the weather becomes disturbed over continents where mountains, valleys, deserts and forests influence local and regional weather.

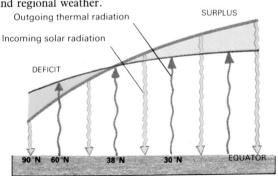

Outgoing thermal radiation

SURPLUS

Incoming solar radiation

DEFICIT

90°N 60°N 38°N 30°N EQUATOR

GLOBAL CIRCULATION

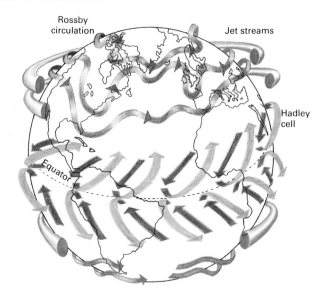

Warm air rising at the Equator, where most solar radiation is received, is carried away southwards and northwards and replaced at the surface by cooler air moving in. The warm air moving away from the Equator starts to cool and descend at around 30 °N and S. This simple circulation, called a Hadley cell, is deflected to the right in the Northern Hemisphere and to the left in the Southern Hemisphere as a result of the Earth's eastwards rotation, giving rise at the surface to the Trade Winds (see **Global winds**). Further towards the poles the circulation grows more complicated. Undulating streams of air (Rossby waves) travel round the globe from west to east, mixing and stirring the atmosphere and bringing warm air towards the poles and cold air towards the Equator. Sheets of cold air coming southward slide under sheets of warmer air moving northward. The surface winds in these latitudes are the prevailing westerlies. The jet streams are narrow ribbons of fast-moving wind also streaming eastwards, encircling the globe high above the surface at sharp discontinuities in temperature, helping to transfer heat between warm tropical air and cold polar air.

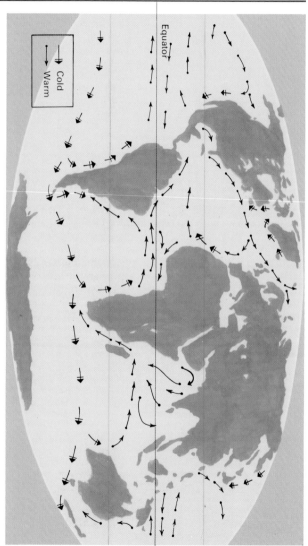

Global currents

The other agents of heat transfer between Equator and poles are the ocean currents. Warm currents like the Gulf Stream in the North Atlantic and the Brazil Current in the South Atlantic flow polewards from the Equator, and cold currents like the icy Labrador Current off the eastern North American coast and the Humboldt Current along the Chilean and Peruvian coast carry cold water away from the poles. The map shows the main ocean currents in the Northern Hemisphere winter. The small picture below shows how they change off India and southeast Asia with the monsoon winds in summer.

The great ocean currents have their origin in the surface winds that blow across the ocean. The Gulf Stream sweeps up the eastern North Atlantic and across to the Arctic as a result of the clockwise winds around the area of persistent high pressure located over the Azores.

Currents near continental coasts can influence the general climate and day to day weather. Warm currents can make an area milder than one would expect for the latitude, as air coming in over the current is warmed and moistened. The warm North Atlantic Drift, the northern continuation of the Gulf Stream, keeps the coasts of Norway free of ice in winter, whereas the St Lawrence River across the Atlantic is blocked by ice. The North Atlantic Drift also brings subtropical climates to pockets of western Ireland, the Scilly Isles and Cornwall.

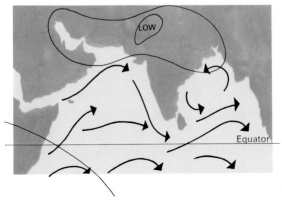

Humidity

As far as weather is concerned, water (H_2O) is the most important ingredient of the atmosphere. Air always contains some water vapour, on average between 1 and 4%, but the amount varies widely. Although water vapour is invisible, we can usually sense when air is moist or humid. Warm moist air makes us feel uncomfortable as it prevents sweat evaporating from our skins and cooling us. Cold moist air feels much more chilling than drier air at the same temperature. The amount of water in the air is known as its **humidity**. The maximum amount of water vapour that air can hold depends on the air temperature. Warm air can hold more water as vapour than can cold air. Air that is holding the maximum possible amount of water at a given temperature is said to be saturated.

Air temp. (°C)	Saturation value (in grams water per cubic metre of air)
30 °C	30.4
10 °C	9.8
0 °C	4.9
−20 °C	1.0

Humidity is often expressed as relatively humidity (R.H.). This is the percentage of water vapour the air is holding at a particular temperature compared with the maximum amount it could contain at that temperature. As air cools its relative humidity increases until it reaches 100% — saturation point. If it is cooled any further the vapour must start to condense out as droplets of water (see **Clouds**). We can see moisture condensing when we breathe out warm moist air into the cold air of a winter's day.

Absolute humidity = 7.27 grams of water vapour per cubic metre			
Temp.	10 °C	16 °C	20 °C	30 °C
R.H. (%)	100	69	54	31

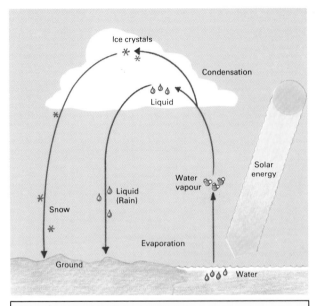

On our planet water can exist as a gas (water vapour), as a liquid, and as a solid (ice). Water is continually evaporating from the Earth's surface into the air where it is held as invisible water vapour which eventually condenses into tiny water droplets to form **clouds**. When condensation takes place in the highest and coldest reaches of the sky, clouds are made of ice crystals. Given the right conditions, clouds return the water to Earth again as rain or snow to complete the water cycle. Evaporation of liquid water to vapour, without a change in temperature, requires a large amount of energy which ultimately comes from the Sun. This energy becomes locked up in the water vapour and is released as latent heat of condensation when vapour condenses. The heat released when large masses of moist air condense helps to generate **cumulonimbus** thunderclouds and **hurricanes**.

WEATHER SYSTEMS

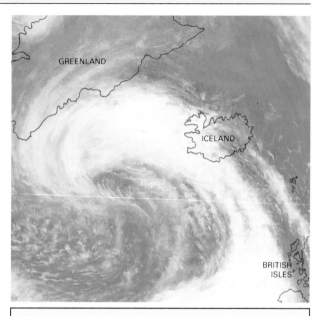

GREENLAND

ICELAND

BRITISH ISLES

When the **atmospheric pressure** at the Earth's surface is plotted, distinct areas of high and low pressure emerge. The areas change from day to day and from season to season, and each has its own distinctive weather patterns. The weather systems based on these areas of low and high pressure determine our day-to-day weather and can extend over thousands of square kilometres. Looking down on the Earth from space, the whirlpools and eddies of thick cloud indicate low-pressure systems (**cyclones**) — the 'lows' or depressions of the **weather map**. Low-pressure systems generally bring unsettled or bad weather, ranging from a few light showers to a raging tropical **hurricane**. High-pressure areas (**anticyclones**), on the other hand, are usually associated with fine weather, especially in summer, but the situation is often more complicated. Large weather systems are generated as a result of the differences in temperature, pressure and humidity between different **air masses**. Where two air masses of different properties meet, a **front** is formed, usually accompanied by clouds and rain. Localized air movements create depressions along the front.

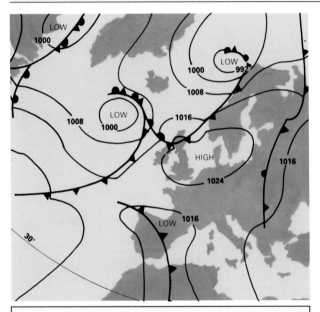

This simplified weather chart, of the sort you will find in your newspapers, shows the disposition of areas of low and high pressure (**cyclones** and **anticyclones**) with their associated fronts for a particular day in summer in the North Atlantic. Charts like these are compiled from data obtained from hundreds of meteorological stations. Points of equal atmospheric pressure are joined by thin lines called isobars, and are drawn here at intervals of 8 millibars. The thick lines represent the surface edges of fronts, estimated from the positions of low and high pressure areas.

moving **cold front**

moving **warm front**

moving **occluded front**

stationary front

isobars with surface pressure in millibars

27

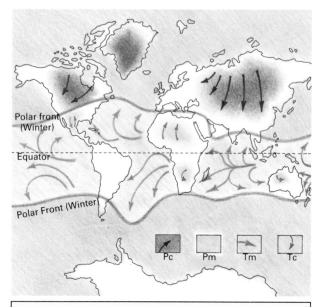

The weather we experience is largely determined by what the air above us is like. Is it warm or cold, moist or dry? The temperature and humidity of air depends on the kind of surface underlying it. Air over warm tropical seas, for example, will always be warmer and moister than air over cold polar regions. Over great areas of the Earth's surface, especially over the oceans and continental interiors, the air is quite uniform in its temperature and humidity in a horizontal direction. These large bodies of air are known as air masses. Although air masses originate over oceans and continental interiors they are often on the move, influencing weather in regions far away and becoming warmer or colder, wetter or drier, as they pass over different surfaces. The main types of air mass are: polar maritime (Pm), polar continental (Pc), tropical maritime (Tm) and tropical continental (Tc). In much simplified terms, Pm air is cold and moist, Pc air is cold and dry, Tm air is warm and wet whereas Tc air is hot and dry. Strong **fronts** are formed where cold polar air and warm tropical air meet.

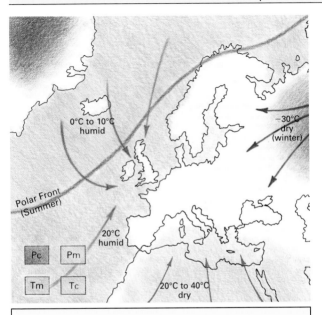

European weather is influenced by four air masses. Our polar maritime (Pm) air originates over the Arctic Ocean and in winter especially it moves south. It may come in from the northwest bringing cool or cold weather, showers and bright intervals. On a longer path over warmer Atlantic waters it picks up more moisture; cool, cloudy, humid weather approaches from the southwest. Pm air sometimes comes from the northeast, bringing cold showery weather with snow or sleet. This air is unpleasantly chilling and is often accompanied by cold north winds. Cold dry polar continental (Pc) air originates over the icy wastes of northern Asia in winter. When it spreads into western Europe it brings bitterly cold, clear weather. Warm moist tropical maritime (Tm) air is centred over the Azores in the north Atlantic and comes in from the southwest. In winter it brings mild cloudy weather. In summer it becomes drier as it sits over Europe and brings clear sunny days. Southern Europe is influenced by tropical continental (Tc) air from the North African deserts. This moves north to give the hot, dry Mediterranean summer.

When a warm air mass meets a cooler one, a distinct boundary — a **front** — is formed, often thousands of kilometres long. The warmer air along the length of the front rises over the cooler air to give a boundary sloping up from the ground and separating warm air from cold. As the warm air rises it cools and a belt of cloud and rain (or snow) is formed. Strong fronts, separating air masses of markedly different temperatures, develop in northern latitudes where cold polar air meets warm tropical air. They are invariably accompanied by rain or snow, often with high winds, and herald a change in the weather as one air mass moves in to replace the other. Weaker fronts, separating air with similar properties, may pass unnoticed except for a slight drop in pressure. The front that influences European weather most is the Polar Front (see p. 29). In summer it generally passes north of the British Isles, but in winter it can move down to southern Europe. Fronts may be stationary, but usually one air mass is moving, pushing the other along. There are three main types of moving front, each accompanied by a typical weather sequence (see **Cold Front**, **Warm Front**, and **Occluded Front**).

CYCLONES (DEPRESSIONS)

A cyclone or depression (the 'Low' of the weather charts) is a distinct area of low surface pressure, with pressure lowest at the centre. It is maintained by air rising at the centre of the low and being removed rapidly by high-level winds blowing away from the centre. At surface level, air is drawn into the depression and is deflected around the centre (see **Coriolis Effect**). Winds therefore blow anticlockwise around a depression in the Northern Hemisphere (clockwise in the Southern Hemisphere). High winds accompany lows when there is a steep pressure gradient from rim to centre and air rushes into the depression. Cyclones are typically thousands of kilometres across and extend vertically throughout the lower troposphere. Low-pressure systems in mid-latitudes are associated with cloud and rain or snow as a result of condensation and precipitation from the rising and cooling air. Over tropical waters cyclones can develop into **hurricanes**. Cyclones are often generated along fronts such as the Polar Front in the northern latitudes see **Occluded Fronts**). 'Valleys' of low pressure called troughs. See p. 27 for symbols.

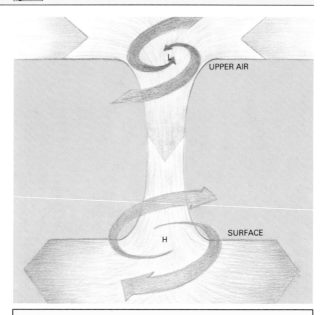

UPPER AIR

SURFACE

Anticyclones (the 'Highs' of the weather charts) are systems of high surface pressure and can extend over vast areas. The air at the centre of an anticyclone is descending towards the surface, becoming compressed and warmed as it sinks, and leaving a low pressure centre in the upper air. At the surface, air flows outwards from the centre of an anticyclone and is deflected as a result of the **Coriolis Effect**. Winds blow clockwise around an anticyclone in the Northern Hemisphere (anticlockwise in the Southern). The pressure gradient from the centre outwards is rarely as steep as in a **cyclone** and winds in anticyclones are usually lighter. Anticyclones are often associated with fine sunny weather as clouds are less likely to form in the sinking warming air. Stationary 'blocking anticyclones' cause the spells of fine but extreme weather experienced from time to time — heatwaves and droughts in summer and bitter cold in winter. Seasonal anticyclones develop in winter over the snow-covered interiors of continents as air is cooled, becomes denser and sinks. The highest surface pressure (1080 mb) ever recorded came from the centre of the winter 'Siberian High'.

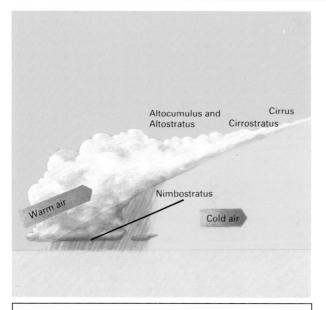

Altocumulus and Altostratus

Cirrus

Cirrostratus

Nimbostratus

Warm air

Cold air

Warm fronts (see **Weather Map** for symbol) occur when warm air moves in to replace a cold air mass. The advancing warm air flows up and over the cold air to form a gently sloping boundary between warm and cool air. This may stretch as much as 1000 km ahead of the surface line of the front. Clouds condense in the rising, cooling air. A warm front is heralded some 48 hours before by **cirrus** clouds, the first sign of the warm air high above, and a fall in pressure. Cirrus gives way to **cirrostratus**. Mid-level **altostratus** clouds follow, giving a leaden overcast sky, or, if the warm air is unstable, a **cirrocumulus** 'mackerel sky'. Dark low-based **nimbostratus** cloud precedes the line of the front itself bringing persistent rain or snow. The rainbelt can be from 250–300 km wide and take 6 hours or more to pass, after which the pressure starts to rise. Warm fronts move fairly slowly, at around 25 kph. If the warm air is unstable, the front may be accompanied by **cumulonimbus** clouds, giving a mixture of steady rain, drizzle and thunder showers. Warm fronts in depressions are often closely followed by a cold front (see **Occluded Front**).

33

COLD FRONT

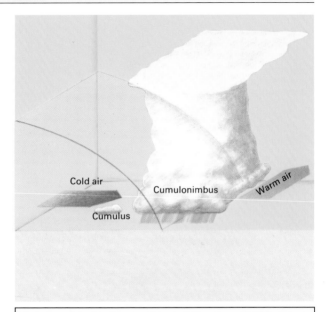

Cold air

Cumulonimbus

Warm air

Cumulus

An advancing cold front (see **Weather Map** for symbol) is typically accompanied by a fall in pressure, followed by heavy showers which clear rapidly to give colder brighter weather and rising air pressure. A cold front forms when a thick wedge of cold air pushes forward under a warm air mass. The warm air is forced sharply up and **cumulonimbus** clouds condense in the rapidly rising and cooling air. They give heavy, sometimes thundery, showers which do not last very long. Cold fronts usually travel faster than **warm fronts**, up to 40–50 kph (25–30 mph) compared to around 25 kph (15 mph). They are also narrower and the whole front has usually passed over within 4–5 hours, hence the saying 'rain before seven, fine before eleven'. Cold fronts may be preceded by high **cirrus** clouds, but these often cannot be seen above the low cloud of the warm air mass and the thick rain-bearing cloud arrives without warning. Slower moving cold fronts give steadier rain from **nimbostratus** clouds mixed with the heavier showers from cumulonimbus clouds. Cold fronts often closely follow warm fronts embedded in depressions (see **Occluded Fronts**).

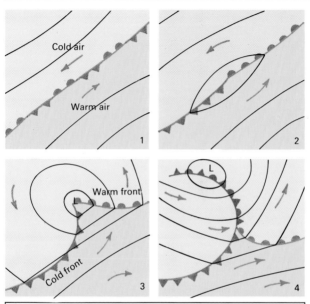

Occluded fronts (see **Weather Map** for symbol) are produced when a **cold front** catches up a **warm front** and they typically form in mid-latitude **cyclones** (depressions). In the Northern Hemisphere, cyclones develop along the front separating the northern cold air mass from warm air to the south (**1**). When the cold air pushes forward under the warmer air at some point (**2**), the front kinks, trapping a sector of warm air between the two arms (**3**). The leading arm becomes a warm front as the warm air in this sector is squeezed up and over the cold air ahead of it by the faster travelling cold front following it. An area of low pressure is formed around the 'kink' as cold air moves rapidly away from it and warm air moves more slowly into it. The cold front usually moves about twice as fast as the warm front and eventually catches it up (**4**), lifting all the warm air aloft and producing an occluded front. The persistent rain typical of a warm front is followed immediately by showers from the cumulonimbus clouds accompanying the cold front, without any intervening fine spell. Once the front has become occluded the depression ceases to grow and pressure starts to equalize.

'Red sky at night, shepherd's delight; red sky in morning, shepherd's warning' is one piece of weather lore known throughout the world. The Chinese will tell you to 'stay at home when the morning sky appears red, but look for a good day's travel when the evening clouds turn crimson'. To the Italians it is 'Ponente rosso, levante adosso'. The saying is one of the more reliable pieces of folklore about the weather, at least in situations where **fronts** with their associated cloud and rain generally travel from west to east, as they often do in western Europe. Vividly coloured skies are produced when the rising or setting Sun shines through a dry, hazy and dusty atmosphere, conditions typical of anticyclonic air. Red skies in the east in the morning suggest that the fine weather has already passed over; any clouds illuminated by the rising Sun are likely to be the forerunners of an advancing front. A red sky in the west in evening is more hopeful. The dry air is on the way bringing fine weather with it.

Clouds

Clouds are the easiest aspect of the weather to study. At any time, about 50% of the Earth's skies are obscured by cloud. So they are almost always there and you just have to step outside and look up at the sky. Sailors and countrymen have always used clouds as weather forecasters, and with a little practice the clouds can tell you a great deal about air conditions and the weather that may be coming (see **Fronts**).

Clouds are made up of microscopic water droplets, or at higher, colder levels, of minute ice crystals. They occur when the water vapour in the air condenses or freezes as air cools. In high-level clouds which are forming at temperatures of around $-40\,°C$, the water is immediately frozen into tiny ice crystals. Although the temperature in even quite low-level clouds can be below $0\,°C$, the water droplets are so small that they can be cooled far below normal freezing point without turning into ice (supercooling).

The water droplets formed by condensation in clouds are mostly no more than 1–50 micrometres (μm)* in diameter. They are very light and remain suspended in the air or fall so slowly that they evaporate before they reach the ground. To fall as rain, droplets must be larger than $100\,\mu$m, at which size they might fall as **drizzle** from very low clouds. True raindrops are much larger — around 1 mm in diameter — and hundreds of thousands of times heavier than cloud droplets. Raindrops are formed inside clouds in various complicated ways (see **Rain**) and only some clouds give rain.

Clouds form in many different situations. Small puffy clouds are generated on the top of up-currents of warm air that are rising above patches of ground heated by the sun. Clouds regularly form over mountains as air is forced to rise up the windward slope, cooling as it rises (see diagram below). **Fronts** and **cyclones** (depressions) are accompanied by extensive cloud as sheets of warm air are lifted high above a surface layer of cold air. **Mist** and **fog** are simply cloud that has formed close to the ground.

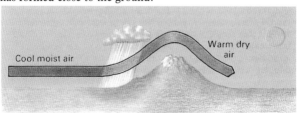

Cool moist air

Warm dry air

* $1\,\mu$m = 0.001 (1/1000) mm.

☁ CLOUD COVER

Over the Earth as a whole, clouds always cover about 50% of the sky. Satellite pictures of the Earth from space show the belt of cloud over equatorial regions, where very warm moist air is continually rising and cooling. To either side of the Equator the air is clearer over deserts and dry grasslands. Whirlpools of cloud indicate **cyclones** (depressions). As well as holding vast amounts of water, which will eventually return to Earth as **rain** or **snow**, clouds help to regulate the temperature. In clear air with no cloud to reflect incoming sunlight, the surface temperature rises rapidly from a minimum just before dawn to a maximum around mid-afternoon. After that, outgoing radiation exceeds incoming and the surface starts to cool down. On a clear night, with no cloud to absorb and re-radiate heat, the surface continues to lose heat into space and rapidly cools. This is why desert nights are so cold after the baking heat of the day. At the other extreme an overcast sky can reflect up to 80% of incoming sunlight. But although daytime is cooler, the cloud also prevents heat being lost, so there is less difference between day and night temperatures in cloudy conditions.

CLOUD FORMATION

CUMULUS CLOUD

Sinking air

SUNLIGHT

Bubble of warm air expands and cools

Warm ground

Clouds are formed when air is cooled past its saturation point (see **Humidity**). Air is cooled adiabatically when it rises and is subject to lower **atmospheric pressure**. It rises on being heated by the ground (as in the diagram above), or when it is forced over an obstacle such as a mountain range or a layer of colder air. Small cumulus clouds typical of a fine day are formed when local heating causes a column of warm air (a thermal) to rise up through the colder surrounding air. The rising air expands as the pressure decreases. Air cools as it expands and so the rising air cools. Cold air can hold less water as vapour than can warm air. If warm moist air is cooled, therefore, it will eventually reach saturation, the point at which it is holding as much water vapour as it can at that temperature. If it is cooled further, water vapour starts to condense as droplets of liquid water, which become visible as cloud. In practice, clouds form before air reaches its saturation point as even the cleanest atmosphere contains particles of dust and salt which provide surfaces on which water condenses more easily.

CLOUD TYPES

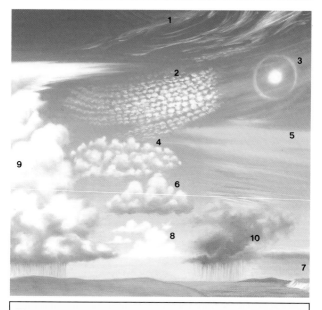

There are two main types of cloud formation. **Cumulus** (or heap) **cloud** is produced by convection: 'bubbles' of air are warmed at the surface and rise rapidly in an unstable atmosphere that tends to encourage upward air movement. **Layer** (or **stratus**) **clouds** are formed when more extensive sheets of moist air are lifted and cooled in a stable stratified atmosphere that tends to prevent upward air movement. Layer clouds form thick or thin sheets, or are broken by wind into billows, ridges and rolls. Convection currents within a sheet of cloud gives formations intermediate between cumulus and layer clouds. The main cloud types were first given their present names in the early 19th century. **Cirrus** (**1**), **cirrocumulus** (**2**) and **cirrostratus** (**3**) are high-level clouds made of ice crystals; **altocumulus** (**4**) and **altostratus** (**5**) are mid-level clouds; **stratocumulus** (**6**) and **stratus** (**7**) are low-level clouds. **Cumulus** clouds range from puffs of fleecy white (**8**) to towering dark thunderclouds (**cumulonimbus** [**9**]) which reach right up to the top of the troposphere. **Nimbostratus** (**10**) clouds are dark low-based rainclouds.

The 'mare's-tails' of the highest reaches of the sky are formed at around 5–11 km and are composed entirely of ice crystals. They may either take the form of small patches of white, silky cloud or be teased out by the winds of the upper atmosphere into fine strands with curled ends. When they stream out spectacularly over the sky they are often the first sign of a storm or an approaching **warm front**. The warm air borne high aloft above the cold resident air starts to condense and freezes instantaneously. The curls and hooks of cirrus are caused as fine trails of ice crystals fall slowly downwards. Ice clouds such as cirrus, **cirrostratus** and **cirrocumulus** form when air reaches its condensation point in temperatures below −40 °C and immediately freezes. Ice clouds tend to grow rather than evaporate after freezing and can be long-lived.

The 'mackerel sky' of the amateur weather forecaster, cirrocumulus is a high-level cloud forming at between 5 and 11 km. It is composed of ice crystals, and develops a regular pattern of bands and rows of tiny white tufts of cloud that looks like mackerel skin. The old rhyme 'mackerel sky; never long wet and never long dry' probably arose as cirrocumulus sometimes precedes a storm or an approaching front bringing unsettled weather.

CIRROSTRATUS (Cs)

Cirrostratus is a transparent veil of ice-crystal cloud forming between 5 and 11 km. It often follows **cirrus** at the approach of a **warm front**, but is difficult to distinguish from haze caused by pollution. However, unlike haze, which is produced by particles of pollutants or by water droplets, the tiny ice crystals of which the cirrostratus veil is composed refract light, characteristically producing haloes around the sun or moon.

ALTOCUMULUS (Ac)

A white or greyish cloud of the middle layers of the troposphere with its base at 2 to 6 km, altocumulus forms higher than **stratocumulus** cloud and can originate from the higher reaches of stratocumulus or large cumulus clouds. It can also appear out of a cloudless sky as air is lifted near an approaching front. Altocumulus is mainly composed of water droplets but may also contain ice crystals in its upper layers. It can take on many forms depending on the movement of the air, including parallel bands and cellular patterns. It often closely resembles stratocumulus, and can be difficult to distinguish, but the individual cloud elements usually seem smaller as they are higher and further away.

Altostratus is the smooth greyish or bluish layer of sometimes streaky cloud that covers all or part of the sky with a base between 2 to 6 km altitude. It is sometimes thin enough for the position of the sun to be seen through it, but not the clear outline. It consists mainly of supercooled water droplets, but ice crystals may form as a result of seeding by crystals falling from higher clouds. It replaces **cirrostratus** as a warm front approaches. If it thickens downwards in cold moist air it can form **nimbostratus**, the raincloud producing persistent rain or snow.

Nimbostratus is a sheet of thick dark grey cloud, with a base between 900 m and 3 km. It is a raincloud, bringing rain or snow depending on the air temperature beneath it. Nimbostratus clouds give a lowering wet grey sky of often persistent rain with detached patches of ragged grey cloud scudding along under the main cloud base, or the almost black sky that heralds snow. They form when a sheet of warm moist air is forced upwards over cold air or over mountains, and when the resulting cloud can thicken enough to produce ice crystals in the upper layers. Nimbostratus typically accompanies **warm fronts** separating two moist air masses. In those conditions, **altostratus** forms first, thickening downwards in the cold wet air.

STRATOCUMULUS (Sc)

Stratocumulus is a common low-level cloud often formed when wind causes turbulence in moist air near the ground, mixing the air vertically and carrying moister air from the surface upwards. Stratocumulus is not a uniform greyish sheet like **stratus** (hence the addition of 'cumulus' to the name), but is composed of more-or-less continuous white or greyish clumps, often arranged in bands or rolls, sometimes separated by clear sky. If the cloud is thicker it appears as light and dark patches. The cloud base ranges from around 400 m to 2 km and this cloud is composed of water droplets. It is quite common in winter when moist, warm air is moving northward. Stratocumulus is not very thick and tends to give only light drizzle (at temperatures above freezing), or light but sometimes persistent snow over hills or in sub-zero temperatures. It can form when **cumulus** clouds hit a stable warm layer and the tops flatten out. The cumulus cloud bases disperse, leaving a layer of stratocumulus. Stratocumulus can thicken downwards when surface air becomes moister, leaving the air above it clear and dry, as one often finds when climbing from cloud in the valley to sunshine higher up.

The featureless low sheet of grey cloud known generally as stratus has a base at around 400 m or lower. It forms in stable air conditions, but where wind at surface level keeps a layer of air below the cloud base well-mixed and too warm for condensation to occur. **Fog** is stratus cloud that has formed at ground level in the absence of turbulence, and conversely, fog lifted off the ground as conditions change becomes stratus. Stratus is rarely thick enough to give rain, but can produce a light **drizzle**, or snow over higher ground. When the sun can be seen through it the outline is clear. Stratus can also form under a true raincloud (**nimbostratus**) when cold rain falls into a warmer layer, evaporating and making the layer moister and colder. It is often seen as ragged clouds (**scud**) blown along by the wind under the base of the raincloud.

The ragged scraps of **stratus** cloud that rise from a valley floor or run along near to the ground under large rainclouds are known as scud or fractus. They form and disperse rapidly. Under a raincloud, scud is formed in patches of lifted and cooled air that become moistened to saturation by the falling rain.

☁ CUMULUS (Cu)

Cumulus clouds are common on sunny days when the ground is strongly heated by the sun. Fleets of these clouds often form, their bases all at the same level (see also **Cloud Streets**). Local heating of the ground produces up-currents of warm air (thermals). Each forms a cauliflower-shaped cloud as the air cools on rising and water vapour condenses. Cumulus clouds have a sharp outline caused by continuous formation of tiny droplets within the cloud, fed by its up-current of warm air, and rapid evaporation at the edges in the drier surrounding air. Small cumulus only last about 15–20 minutes, evaporating as they drift away from the source of the warm air that feeds them. Cumulus typically starts to form in mid-morning as the ground warms up, is most extensive in mid-afternoon and disperses as the ground cools down. The cloud base is usually around 700 m, but may be as low as 500 m or as high as 2000 m. The height of the cloud top is determined by the height at which the rising air has cooled to the temperature of the surrounding air and is no longer buoyant. Cumulus clouds are separated by descending air compensating for the up-currents.

Over open country **cumulus** clouds often line up in a row which is called a cloud street. These formations are sometimes the result of a succession of clouds being generated in the moist air carried upwards by a thermal and then moving downwind. On a sunny day over a flat uniform surface, regular parallel streets of clouds may be formed, extending into the distance as far as the eye can see. These are the result of the pattern of updraughts and downdraughts created by general heating of the land and the direction of the breeze. On satellite photographs large areas of cloud streets are often spotted over the seas.

Small fair-weather **cumulus** can develop into much larger cumulus clouds — known as cumulus congestus. They are among the most fascinating clouds to watch as the persistent up-currents of air within the cloud produce continually changing bubbles and puffs on the upper surface. They develop in conditions where the air inside the cloud remains warmer than the surrounding air and so the cloud remains lighter than its surroundings and continues to grow upwards, fed by the strong up-currents of air within it. These rise at speeds of up to 20 metres per second. Cumulus congestus tops can reach up to 3– 5 km. They sometimes flatten when they meet a stable warm layer of air, but unlike a fully developed **cumulonimbus** cloud, into which they can develop, this top is not frozen. In mid-latitude climates cumulus congestus clouds rarely give rain but can give light showers. In the tropics, however, large cumulus clouds developing from very moist air are the source of heavy rain (see **Warm Rain**).

If you watch large **cumulus congestus** clouds rising you may be lucky enough to catch sight of the elusive pileus cloud. A small thin cloud with a smooth domed upper surface, it forms transitorily above rising cumulus. When cumulus is rising towards a horizontally moving air layer above it, the rising air ahead of it makes a small dent in the layer before it penetrates it. If the air is sufficiently moist a small cloud forms as air flows up and into the crest of this dent. Soon the cumulus top catches up with it and after draping the top for a few minutes, the pileus cloud disappears into the mass of rising cloud.

In extremely unstable atmospheric conditions huge dense cumulus clouds form, white at the edges but very dark at the base and towering the whole height of the troposphere. They grow from large cumulus clouds with bases between 500 m and 2 km and tops at between 3 and 6 km. In the unstable conditions, the air within these clouds is warmer than the surrounding air and so the cloud continues to grow, with very strong convectional up-currents within it. Heat produced as the massive amounts of water vapour condense helps feed the updraughts of warm air. The top of the cloud freezes to ice crystals, which grow steadily as water droplets are swept upwards and stick to them. The bubbling dome characteristic of growing cumulus becomes flattened once it freezes and often spreads out in a wide plume (the anvil) on the prevailing high-level winds. Fully-developed cumulonimbus clouds are thunderclouds, which bring heavy **rain** or **hail** showers and **thunderstorms**.

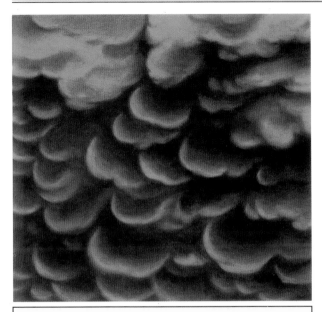

The underside of the spreading anvil of a **cumulonimbus** stormcloud is sometimes a mass of rounded hanging pouches of falling ice crystals that are revealed when low sun strikes the undersurface of the anvil. The pouches appear on the cloud after or towards the end of the storm and are called mamma from their obvious resemblance to breasts. They can also appear on the base of the raincloud as falling small droplets cluster together.

In the evening after a warm sunny day, tall thin cumulus 'towers' can sometimes be seen sprouting from a thin **altocumulus** cloud layer forming over low hills, a valley or a narrow stretch of water. If the towers are ascending into dry air they quickly evaporate into fleecy 'floccus'. Thin towers can sometimes also be seen sprouting from the top and sides of large cumulus clouds. They each represent an up-current of warm air. Altocumulus castellanus indicates unstable air and thus sometimes precedes heat-generated thunderstorms.

MOUNTAIN CLOUDS
Cloud caps

Clouds of all sorts are especially frequent in the mountains. The uneven and varied land surface and high altitudes create excellent conditions for the formation of both convective (**cumulus**) clouds and layer clouds (see **Clouds**). Mountains also have some cloud formations typically their own. The cloud that often hangs almost permanently over some mountains, especially those near the sea, is caused by the uplift and cooling of moist air when it meets the windward slope. Cloud forms on the higher windward slopes, often also shedding its moisture as rain or snow. Once over the summit the air starts to descend. It is compressed by the increasing pressure and starts to warm up. Having shed most of its moisture it is usually also drier by this time and so the cloud cap does not extend far below the summit on the leeward side. Although a cloud cap seems stationary, it is not the same cloud all the time but is continually being formed in the airflow. Clouds formed by forced lifting of air by an obstacle such as a mountain range are known as orographic clouds.

A lens-shaped (lenticular) cloud can form high above a mountain when a stream of high-level moist air rises as it flows over the summit. If there are several layers of moist air, piles of lenticular clouds are formed looking uncannily like 'flying saucers', as in this illustration of lenticular clouds in Antarctica. A less spectacular series of lenticular clouds is formed when a stable airflow forced up a mountain slope forms waves after it clears the summit, the so-called 'lee waves'. The descending air is carried along on these waves and cooled as it rises to the crests. If it is cooled to saturation, a train of shallow lenticular clouds, steadily decreasing in size, can form to leeward of the mountains.

MOUNTAIN CLOUD
Banner cloud

High isolated peaks do not present enough surface area to the wind to force it to flow over the summit. The airstream divides below the summit and the turbulence caused makes the air rise slightly to leeward of the mountain. With a moist airstream this rise is sufficient to form a cloud which streams out with the wind and gradually evaporates from the base to form a roughly triangular or banner shape.

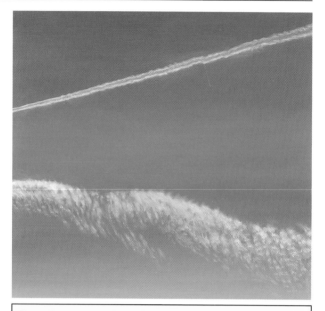

Contrails (an abbreviation of condensation trails) are the straight lines of cloud that form in the wake of an aircraft. They are produced by condensation of the water vapour emitted from the aircraft's engines (water vapour is a product of fuel combustion). In dry air they disperse quickly but in moist air they persist for a long time, gradually thinning out and becoming less distinct. The space between the engines and the start of the contrail is a result of the air coming from the engines being too hot to condense immediately. Distrails (dissipation trails) are paths of clear air evaporated from a cloud by the heat of the engines as an aircraft passes through it.

Fog and mist are in many respects simply clouds that form immediately above the ground, and like clouds, they occur for different reasons in different situations. In all cases a layer of air next to the surface must cool below its condensation point to produce fog. The water vapour condenses as tiny droplets which remain suspended in the air. Fog and mist drops are very small. Fog drops are similar in size to those in clouds — 1–50 micrometres (μm)* in diameter; mist drops are even smaller, less than 1 μm across. Fog and mist form when the air is fairly calm, but not usually absolutely still. In meteorological terms fog is any atmospheric condition that obscures surface visibility to less than 1 km; motorway accidents and airport disruption are usually caused by thick fog — visibility worse than 200 m. Mist is thinner, reducing visibility to between 1 and 2 km. A similar condition due to dust or smoke in the atmosphere is called haze. When moist air close to the ground is cooled in completely still air, **dew** often forms. When the air and ground cool to below 0 °C, **frost** is likely as the moisture in the air freezes out as ice crystals.

* 1 μm = 0.001 (1/1000) mm.

Fog that forms in river valleys and damp hollows and over low-lying land at night is produced when still moist air is chilled as the ground under it loses heat during the night. It is therefore the result of radiational cooling, from which it gets its name. Radiation fog only develops over land and is most common when nights are long — in autumn and winter — when it can last all through the following day and even not lift for days. In summer the sun is generally warm enough to shift it early in the morning. A clear sky, so that the ground cools right down at night, and only a very slight movement of the air (around 1–3 metres per second) are needed to produce it. If the air is completely still, however, only a very thin layer of fog forms at ground level; too much wind and the fog is lifted to form low **stratus** cloud. Radiation fog is often patchy, depending for its formation on the contours of the land and whether the land surface loses heat readily. It tends to gather in hollows and valleys because air becomes denser and heavier as it cools and runs down to the bottom of a slope. A layer of radiation fog can be up to 300 m deep, but is usually less.

Fog at sea is usually the result of warm moist air moving slowly over a cold surface. The air cools and water vapour condenses. Fog produced in this way is called advection fog to distinguish it from **radiation fog**. It is common at sea when warm moist air moves over a cold current, or when warm tropical air moves in over colder waters. The regular fog off the Californian coast is the result of warm moist air from the Pacific rolling in over the cold Californian coast current. Advection fog is very similar to **stratus** cloud, but is produced when the air is calmer close to the ground. The air immediately above the surface remains cold and the 'cloud' stays as a layer on the ground. Wind speeds of about 4.5 m per second are ideal conditions for advection fog and it generally makes a layer around 100 m thick. Fog coming in from the sea often clears when it reaches the warmer land surface. When advection fog forms over land it tends to disperse during the day as the land warms up, and reforms at night. Daytime warming or increased wind speeds can also lift the fog off the ground to produce stratus cloud. Hill fogs are sometimes caused this way.

STEAM FOG

Steam fog or 'Arctic smoke' is the result of cold air moving over warm water. For steam fog to form there has to be a large temperature difference (at least 10 °C) between water and air. Evaporation from the warmer water into the already cold air saturates it almost immediately and the vapour condenses. This type of fog is often seen in the Arctic when cold air from above ice and snow blows over relatively warm water and the surface appears to steam. It rarely forms a layer more than about 15 m thick and is often much thinner. A similar phenomenon is seen over sun-warmed roads in summer after a sudden shower, and when cold air moves over the warmer water of lakes and rivers.

SMOG

Smog is a combination of smoke or other pollutants and fog. Now that the 'London' smogs caused by smoke and sulphur dioxide from domestic coal fires are a thing of the past, the worst pollution threat to human health and comfort in cities comes from the exhaust fumes of motor vehicles. Exhaust emissions contain carbon monoxide, oxides of nitrogen, various hydrocarbons, lead (from leaded petrol), and small amounts of SO_2 as well as carbon dioxide. In hot sunny conditions the effects of exhaust pollution are made worse by the formation of 'photochemical smog'. Sunlight acts on nitric oxides to form ozone and nitrogen dioxide. Together with formaldehyde and peroxyacetyl nitrate (PAN), these gases irritate eyes and lungs and also damage plants. Visibility is reduced as the increased number of particles in the air create haze, and act as nuclei on which moisture condenses into fog and mist. The photochemical smogs of Los Angeles and San Francisco persist for days as the polluted air is trapped under an upper warm layer (an inversion). Cars in California are fitted by law with catalytic converters which reduce emissions of some pollutants.

The tiny droplets of dew that typically bejewel cobwebs and leaves on a still autumn morning are formed when the ground loses heat at night, cooling the air immediately in contact with the ground down to the dew point. At this point water vapour in the air condenses onto any cold surface, just as a glass of cold water will cool the surrounding air enough to form condensation on the outside. A clear night and still air are ideal conditions for a dewy morning. Dew on grass is sometimes confused with drops of water produced by the plants themselves in the process of guttation and which cannot evaporate into the surrounding water-saturated air. Guttation drops are large drops usually hanging at the tip of the leaf, whereas the smaller dewdrops cover the flat surface. The heaviest dews occur when moist warm air moves in over surfaces that are already very cold, as sometimes happens when the weather suddenly changes after a cold spell. In places with adequate rainfall, dew provides a very small proportion of water returning to the ground, but it can be an essential source of moisture for plant and animal life where there is little rainfall.

Frost is likely to form when air and ground are colder than 0 °C. When air that is being cooled in contact with cold ground reaches its saturation point at sub-zero temperatures, the water vapour in the air freezes to form needle-like crystals of ice which are deposited on the ground as a sparkling white layer of hoar frost. Hoar frost is most common after a clear calm cold night. The delicate tracings of fern frost that form on the insides of window panes in very cold weather are the result of crystallization of supercooled water drops. The first ice crystals trigger off a chain reaction to make the feather-like patterns. A 'black frost' (when air temperature is less than 0 °C) can occur without visible signs of hoar frost when air is very dry and is not saturated at sub-zero temperature. It is very damaging to plants. Another dangerous manifestation of frost is rime. This is a covering of ice that builds up on surfaces when they are exposed to supercooled fog (fog in which the water droplets are colder than 0 °C but have not frozen). On contact with a surface, supercooled fog freezes and crusts of ice may build up. Icing on aircraft is due to this phenomenon.

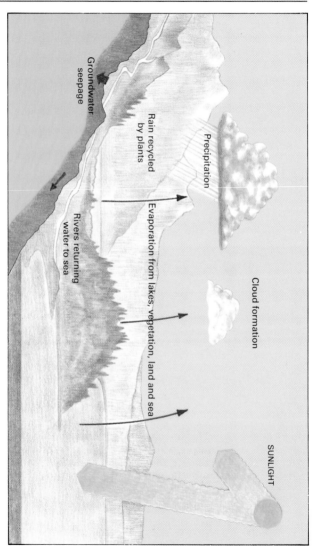

Groundwater seepage

Rain recycled by plants

Precipitation

Evaporation from lakes, vegetation, land and sea

Rivers returning water to sea

Cloud formation

SUNLIGHT

The Water Cycle

Although rain and its winter equivalent, snow, are often unwelcome, they are essential to life. They replenish the moisture in the ground and fill the lakes and rivers that we depend on for water. Precipitation, the meteorological term for water fall-out in all its forms, is the final turn in the cycle that starts when water is evaporated from oceans, lakes, the ground and vegetation by the Sun's energy. Clouds form when the moist air is forced to rise and cool. But not all clouds produce rain or snow. Rain clouds occur along the cold and warm **fronts** in **cyclones**, where a layer of warmer air rises above cold air, cooling and condensing as it ascends. Local showers and storms are produced from large **cumulonimbus** clouds, which arise by convection. Rain clouds are also formed when moist air is forced to rise as it meets high ground (orographic clouds). As illustrated opposite, moisture-laden air from over the oceans moves in over the coast. Meeting high ground it rises and the water vapour within it condenses into cloud. In the right conditions the cloud becomes thick enough to produce rain (or snow if the temperature is cold enough). Because most of the rain tends to fall on the coastal slopes and summits, the landward slopes of coastal mountain ranges are usually much drier. Continental interiors in mid-latitudes, away from the equatorial rain forest belts, are also drier than coastal regions.

Rainfall statistics gathered throughout the year at one location give the 'point rainfall' for that site. Two of the wettest places in the world are Mt Wai-'ale-'ale on the Hawaiian island of Kauai, with more than 1100 cm of rain per annum, and Cherrapungi, in the mountains of Assam, with well over 1000 cm of rain per annum, almost all of it in the monsoon season in late spring and summer. In contrast the wetter parts of Europe only average around 142 cm of rain per annum.

Water is stored in natural reservoirs — in rocks, soil, lakes, rivers and oceans. The absence of rain or snow that would normally fall is a **drought**, which can occur at any time of the year and in any climate. In contrast, more rain than the terrain is adapted to causes **flooding**.

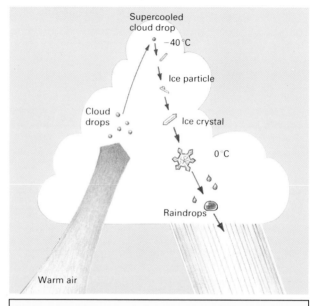

In most types of cloud the individual water droplets do not survive long enough to form drops large and heavy enough to reach the ground before evaporating. Rain falling from **nimbostratus** or **cumulonimbus** clouds has in fact started its journey as snowflakes originating high in the frozen cloud top. There cloud drops freeze into tiny ice crystals. They collide with and freeze the small supercooled cloud drops and grow into snowflakes. Once they have grown heavy enough the snowflakes start falling, melting as they pass through the warmer layers of the cloud. These droplets are large enough to keep falling and collide with and gather smaller cloud drops to them. Drops that reach a size of 1 mm or more by the time they reach the base of the cloud fall as rain. Because of their resistance to the air, falling raindrops are not tear-shaped, as pictured in cartoons, but resemble small buns. The largest raindrops are around 3 mm in diameter and fall at a speed of 8 m per second. The occasional very large raindrops are likely to be hailstones or snowflakes that have melted just before reaching the ground.

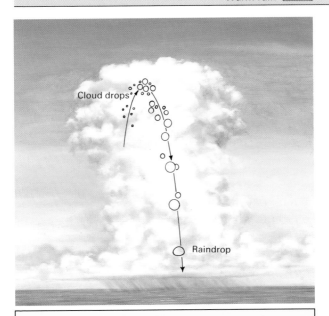

Cloud drops

Raindrop

In the tropics, rain falls from clouds whose tops remain unfrozen. Updraughts in large moist tropical clouds are slow but steady; cloud droplets remain in the cloud long enough (30–40 minutes) to grow large and coalesce with other drops to form raindrops. Rain produced in this way is often called 'warm' rain to distinguish it from rain originating from ice crystals. Even outside the tropics, warm rain sometimes falls from large **cumulus** clouds in evening, as the cooling air slows down convection. This is the usual explanation of evening showers that appear after a fine day of cumulus clouds but no rain. Cumulus clouds forming over the sea can also give warm rain, as upward convection currents over water are weaker than over land, so that cloud droplets are not swept out of the cloud to evaporate but have time to grow.

ACID RAIN

Sulphur dioxide released by the burning of fossil fuels (particularly oil and coal) becomes transformed in the air and in clouds into sulphurous and sulphuric acids. Harmful to animals and plants, they can be carried long distances and are eventually washed out in rain. Acid rain gradually acidifies lakes, rivers and soils on which it falls. The effects of acid rain on the environment in Europe first came to notice in western and southern Scandinavia where lakes had become acid and lifeless. Acid rain has also been blamed for the widespread damage to forests in central Europe. Sulphur dioxide also contributed in the past to the choking 'London fogs' (see **Smog**), that claimed thousands of lives. The use of smokeless fuels has made the air of our cities much cleaner in this respect, and there are stricter controls on the amount of sulphur dioxide that can be emitted from power plants and factories. Acid in the air in cities (in this case mainly from nitrous oxides in car exhausts) is also responsible for damage to limestone and marble buildings, such as the Parthenon in Athens.

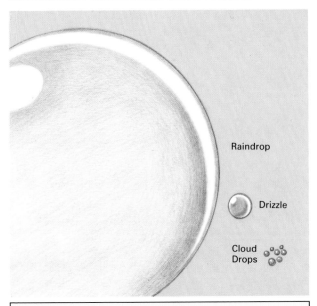

Raindrop

Drizzle

Cloud Drops

Low thin clouds that cannot give rain can sometimes give a fine drizzle. Drizzle drops are small (100–400 micrometres [μm]⋆ diameter) and drizzle is quite distinct from light rain, where the drops are proper raindrops — 1 mm or more across. Drizzle only falls from very low cloud. This is because a water droplet 400 μm across can only fall 100 m or so through clear air before it evaporates. In contrast, a raindrop of 1 mm across can fall 1 km before evaporating. Drizzle usually falls through cool moist air which slows evaporation. Neither rain nor drizzle can fall from thin clouds composed only of very small drops, and they cannot fall from high-based clouds, as the falling drops or crystals simply evaporate before reaching the ground. Trails of ice crystals (virga) are sometimes seen falling from high clouds and disappearing before they reach the ground.

⋆ 1 μm = 0.001 (1/1000) mm.

Rainfall is considered light when it falls at less than 0.5 mm per hour, moderate at 0.5–4 mm per hour and heavy at over 4 mm per hour. Showers are short bursts of rain, often heavy but generally soon over. They usually fall from large **cumulonimbus** clouds. These occur at and behind cold fronts, which therefore bring showery weather rather than persistent rain. Large cumulus clouds can hold an enormous amount of water, which empties over the land suddenly and with great force. Isolated thunderclouds can give heavy showers of such intensity that they cause local flooding. Some exceptional cloudbursts have been recorded: in Montana, over 30 cm of rain fell in 42 minutes, a rate of more than a centimetre a minute; in Hampstead in London, 17 cm of rain in 2½ hours caused flash floods. Showers usually mean that a cloud is nearing the end of its life, as the warm updraughts that feed it are overwhelmed by the downward rush of cold air and rain. Light showers can fall from quite small cumulus clouds, especially those that develop over the sea where convection currents are weak (see **Warm Rain**).

Floods occur for many reasons. On low-lying coasts, the greatest
danger is from **storm surges** accompanying hurricanes or
depressions, and made greater by high winds and high tides.
Inland, natural and man-made water courses and reservoirs are
adapted to cope with the average rainfall and become overloaded
if too much falls in a short space of time. The Florence floods of
early November 1966, in which many art treasures were lost or
damaged, were caused by the River Arno overflowing its banks
after a day of continuous rain following an unusually wet
October which had already filled the river almost brimfull. Less
severe flash floods often occur in towns and cities when sudden
localized cloudbursts overload drains, which become blocked
with debris. The effects of heavy rain in mountain regions are
often made worse by landslides and mudslides, especially if the
area is naturally dry and treeless or where deforestation or
development have removed the protective cover of vegetation
which would normally soak up the water. Flooding can also
occur if the soil, which normally absorbs large amounts of water,
is baked hard by drought or frozen solid in winter.

In meteorological terms, drought is an absence of the rain that would normally fall and so the definition of a drought will vary from place to place. In Europe we usually receive enough rain for our needs, although it does not always fall exactly when and where it is wanted. But from time to time dry spells of hot summer weather turn into a real drought. An 'absolute drought' in western Europe (and other regions where rain is expected all the year round) is a period of 15 or more consecutive days without rain (or with less than 0.2 mm per day). Summer droughts in Europe occur when an **anticyclone** stays stationary over the region for a long period, blocking the path of the Atlantic depressions that normally bring rain. A blocking anticyclone over northwestern Europe caused an exceptional drought in 1976, whereas the Mediterranean had an unusually wet summer as the depressions were diverted southwards. In other parts of the world severe drought is a regular occurrence and contributes to the continuing famine in Africa. The lands around the Sahara, where life depends on a seasonal rainfall of 200–500 mm, have had several cycles of rainless years.

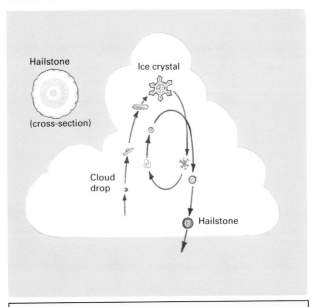

Hailstone
(cross-section)

Ice crystal

Cloud drop

Hailstone

Thunderclouds (**cumulonimbus**) sometimes give hail and not rain, even in summer. Hailstones are more or less round hard pellets of ice, and in cross-section layers of clear and opaque ice can often be seen. Hailstones are formed as ice crystals are repeatedly tossed up and down in the cloud by violent air currents. They coalesce with supercooled cloud drops, which freeze to form layers of ice around the original nucleus. Clear ice forms when the hailstone is in the lower, warmer, part of the cloud, where water freezes fairly slowly; the opaque layers are acquired nearer the top of the cloud where the drops freeze instantaneously on contact. Hailstones are usually 5–50 mm in diameter but larger stones, up to 190 mm across have fallen. Severe hailstorms are commonest over the plains in continental interiors, where large active thunderclouds are common. Soft pellets of ice (known as 'graupel') are snow that has melted and partly refrozen. They consist of a soft core surrounded by a thin layer of ice. Small insects and even frogs have formed the nucleus of hailstones, having been swept up into the cloud by strong up-currents.

SNOW

The snow that transforms even the dreariest landscape starts high in the frozen tops of large thick clouds. Minute ice crystals form in the very low temperatures there (below $-40\,°C$) and crystallize more vapour to them to build beautifully symmetrical 'snowflakes'. When these become heavy enough they start to fall. If the temperature is below $0\,°C$ all the way down from the top of the cloud to the ground, the snowflakes reach the ground intact, growing larger on their way down. Snow falls even in the tropics, but only over high mountains. Dry powdery snow falls when temperatures are so low that the falling crystals do not melt and refreeze when they touch and so do not form large soft flakes. It is very light and extremely penetrating but is ideal for skiing. Wet snow, in contrast, is composed of crystals that have melted and refrozen together to form soft flakes. It makes good snowballs and snowmen as it sticks together easily. Wet snow falls more commonly in maritime regions and dry snow over continental interiors. Some 900 mm depth of dry snow, compared with 175 mm of wet snow, is required to provide the equivalent of 25 mm rain.

Ice crystals and 'snowflakes' come in a variety of forms —
needles, hexagons, columns, prisms and six-pointed stars —
depending on the temperature of the air through which they fall.
They all have a six-sided symmetry however, which stems from
the molecular structure of frozen water. Snowflakes are formed
of many of these microscopic hexagonal crystals frozen together.
The star-shaped crystals popularly called 'snowflakes' are known
technically as dendritic crystals. They are formed in fairly moist
air at temperatures around −15 °C. No two crystals are identical
and the individual shapes are the result of the growth of the
crystal through a complicated sequence of evaporation,
condensation, sublimation (direct conversion of water vapour to
ice) and deposition around a tiny hexagonal ice nucleus.

A snowstorm becomes a blizzard in strong winds (50 kilometres per hour [kph] or more). The snow drives horizontally, piling up in huge drifts when it comes up against an obstacle. This means that the same amount of snowfall in blizzard conditions usually creates many more problems than when it forms an even cover. Deep lanes are filled to the top, leaving neighbouring fields swept bare, and drifts of hard, wind-packed snow block city streets. Blizzards may also be caused by strong winds whipping up already fallen snow, as in the Arctic and Antarctic. In more temperate regions, the source of air for a blizzard is originally moist and fairly warm, as very cold air cannot hold enough moisture to produce heavy persistent snow. The combination of cold and wind in a blizzard is very dangerous to human beings, as the wind chill factor causes air temperatures to drop. Properly clothed, a person is safe in temperatures down to around −28°C if it is calm. But if a wind of 50 kph is blowing, the temperature experienced drops from −28 to −60°C. There is then a danger of frostbite and of death from exposure, and bare flesh rapidly freezes.

When mild weather comes to snow-covered hills and mountains, melting loosens the snow on the slopes. Masses of snow break loose and slide downhill in an avalanche. A whole layer of snow can break away along a fault, or a rush of snow may fan out from a single point; overhanging cornices are also prone to break off. Avalanches often also occur on steep slopes in heavy snow storms as the slope cannot carry the extra weight of snow. Snow ready to move can be set off by wind, the movement of skiers or even by a sharp noise. Avalanches move fast, rapidly engulfing everything in their path. Snow can move at up to 80 kph (50 mph) along the ground and at higher speeds becomes airborne. Avalanches are particularly dangerous in heavily populated mountain areas such as the Alps.

Winds

Winds are the horizontal movement of air as it flows from an area of high pressure to an area of lower pressure. On the global scale, the air in the lower atmosphere is circulating continually as heat is redistributed from equator to poles (see **General Circulation**). As these great air movements sweep the surface of the globe, they become the reliable **Global Winds** that blow steadily over the oceans. At a more local level, winds are generated in many different ways. Air is twisted around **cyclones** (areas of low pressure) and **anticyclones** (areas of high pressure) (see **Coriolis effect**), is forced up over mountains and funnelled through valleys (see **Local Winds**). In cities and towns, tall buildings create their own local circulation. **Breezes** are often generated by localized heating and cooling of the air as the land warms up during the day and cools down at night. Absolutely windless days are rare in most places, and when they occur, are usually associated with the presence of a large area of stationary high pressure. In contrast, the autumn and winter **gales and storms** that hit the western coasts of Europe accompany deep depressions (cyclones) travelling in from the Atlantic. The strongest winds are generated in **hurricanes** and **tornadoes** (estimated at up to 650 kph), and in gusts on high mountains (up to 350 kph). Winds are described in terms of their speed and the direction from which they are blowing. A westerly wind, for example, blows from the west towards the east. The windiest place in the world is Eastern Adelie land on the coast of Antarctica. Strong winds blow continuously down off the icecap towards the sea, reaching hurricane-force (more than 120 kph) on one day out of three.

Wind speeds are described in different ways in different countries: in metres per second, kilometres per hour, miles per hour, or knots (nautical miles* per hour) or a Force number on the Beaufort Scale (see pages 124/125). The speed of the wind depends on the steepness of the pressure gradient that is creating it. The steeper the gradient the greater the wind speed. On the **weather map**, closely spaced isobars indicate a steep pressure gradient and a strong wind. Because of the Coriolis effect, winds blow along the isobars and not directly across them from high to low pressure as one might expect.

* 1 nautical mile = 1852 metres.

CORIOLIS EFFECT

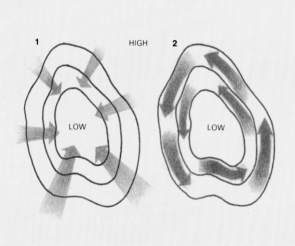

Air naturally flows from an area of high pressure to an area of lower pressure. Looking at the low pressure system illustrated here, we might therefore expect the wind to blow into the depression straight across the isobars (**1**). But instead, the wind blows round the centre of the depression parallel to the isobars (**2**). This happens because the Earth's eastwards rotation deflects all horizontal air movement to the right in the Northern Hemisphere (and to the left in the Southern Hemisphere) (the Coriolis effect). Winds therefore blow anticlockwise around **cyclones** (low pressure areas) and clockwise around **anticyclones** (high pressure areas) in the Northern Hemisphere and the other way round in the Southern. This gives us the rule (Buys Ballot's Law) that if you stand with your back to the wind, the area of low pressure will always be on your left (in the Northern Hemisphere). A shift in the direction of the wind often means a change in the weather. A backing wind is one shifting in a counterclockwise direction and is a sign of low-pressure areas and approaching storms. Veering winds are shifting clockwise and are generally a sign of high pressure and fine weather.

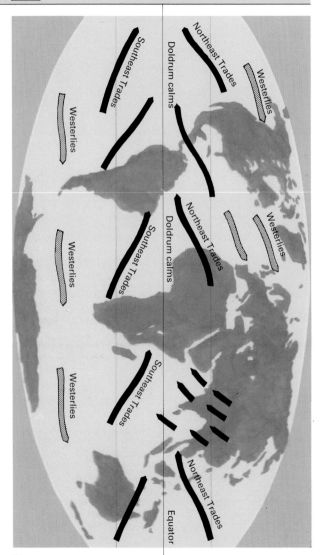

Global Winds

The pattern of surface winds is a reflection of the **general circulation** of the atmosphere and of the distribution of persistent areas of high and low pressure. The map shows the main winds that blow in winter. At the Equator are the doldrums, where winds rarely blow and where, in the days of sailing ships, vessels could become becalmed for weeks. Between 30° North and South over the Atlantic and the Pacific are the belts of the Trade Winds, blowing steadily from the northeast in the Northern Hemisphere and the southeast in the Southern for most of the year. Around 30°N is a sub-tropical belt of high pressure with little surface wind (the 'Horse Latitudes' of the old sailing ships). To the north the polar westerlies blow strongly across the Atlantic and the Pacific in winter, and carry weather out of the Atlantic to western Europe and out of the Pacific onto the west coast of North America. A strong westerly wind blows around the Southern Ocean all the year round, and these latitudes are often known as the Roaring Forties.

In some parts of the world, changes in the location of high and low pressure centres from winter to summer result in a seasonal change of prevailing winds. The most famous of these are the monsoon winds of the Indian sub-continent. On the large map opposite you can see the situation in winter. Dry winds blow from the North, from the high pressure area over snow-covered northern Asia. In summer, as illustrated below, the area of high pressure collapses and moisture-laden winds, the monsoons, blow in from the south, bringing long-awaited rain to the Indian sub-continent.

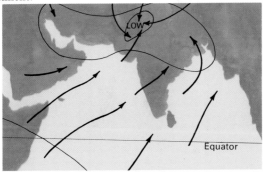

Breezes are winds of up to 50 kilometres per hour (kph) (Force 1–6 on the Beaufort Scale, see pages 124/125). The strongest breezes (Force 6) set large branches swaying and blow umbrellas inside out. At sea they raise fair-sized waves with long white crests and some blowing spray. The illustration shows a Force 5 breeze (30–39 kph). A gentler breeze often blows from sea to shore, especially on tropical coasts, on a hot sunny day. This sea breeze reaches speeds of up to 17 kph (around Force 3) and is caused by the land warming up and cooling down more quickly than the sea. On a sunny day, air above land is rapidly warmed. The warm air rises, and cooler air from over the sea moves in at surface level to take its place. Sea breezes outside the tropics are strongest when the temperature difference between land and sea is greatest — in spring and early summer when the land is warming up but the sea is still cool. Daily warming and cooling also cause the typical reversal of wind direction in morning and evening in mountain valleys. The sides of the valley are warmed in daytime causing a warm wind to blow up the slope. At night, cold air flows down the valley sides.

Winds between 62 and 87 kilometres per hour (kph) are gales (Force 8–9 on the Beaufort Scale; see pages 124/125) and winds above 88 kph are storm force winds (Force 10–11). The picture illustrates a Force 8 gale (62–74 kph), which blows whole trees about and tears off twigs and leaves. Above 119 kph winds officially become hurricane-force (Force 12) as such wind speeds are rarely maintained outside tropical cyclonic storms (**hurricanes**). True hurricanes are only generated over tropical waters; the hurricane-force winds that hit southern Britain and northern France in October 1987 and January 1990, causing immense damage, were part of a deep depression (see **Cyclone**) moving up the Channel from the Atlantic. Gales and storm-force winds outside the tropics are almost always associated with depressions, and are often known as 'frontal storms', as the depressions are generated along the **fronts** between warm and cold **air masses**. Gales and storms are regularly encountered at sea, but storm-force winds are seldom experienced inland.

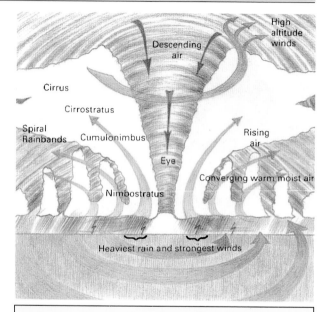

Hurricanes are revolving systems of intensely low pressure, which form only over tropical seas and in which wind speeds often exceed 160 kilometres per hour (kph). A tropical storm is raised to hurricane status when steady winds exceed 119 kph. Wind speed increases towards the centre, the 'eye' of the hurricane, which is an area of relative calm around 11 km across. Pressure in the centre is typically around 950 mb but may be as low as 870 mb. The whole system measures 80–800 km in diameter. Hurricanes only form over tropical waters as they require a continual source of very moist warm air. Officially called 'tropical revolving storms', they are known as hurricanes in the Caribbean, typhoons in the China Sea, tropical cyclones in the Indian Ocean and Willy-Willies off Australia. Air is thrown outwards from the centre to spiral upwards in a ring around the eye. A wall of towering **cumulonimbus** clouds up to 11 km high surrounds the eye, giving torrential rain. As a hurricane passes over, an observer experiences a furious storm blowing from one direction followed by a calm period, after which the storm returns, blowing in the opposite direction.

A tornado is an intense whirlwind, spinning down in a funnel from the base of a large thundercloud or **hurricane** and often accompanied by rain or hail and lightning. Where the tip touches the ground it cuts a swathe of devastation a metre to a kilometre across, and sucks up dust and debris. Wind speed inside a tornado is difficult to measure, but may reach around 660 kph, the greatest wind speed encountered on Earth. The tip of a tornado may lift from the ground and lower again several times during its path. Tornadoes usually spin anticlockwise in the Northern Hemisphere, and clockwise in the Southern. They can travel at some speed and may continue for hundreds of kilometres. The hollow opening in the centre of the funnel is around 15–30 m wide at the tip. Devastating tornadoes occur most frequently on the central plains of the United States from Texas to Kansas in late spring, where hundreds of tornadoes each year are not unknown. Tornadoes cause damage by the direct impact of the wind magnified by its twisting and also by the intensely low pressure in the centre. As it passes over, buildings explode outwards as the air is sucked out.

WATERSPOUTS

Tornado-type whirlwinds occurring over the sea create waterspouts. The low pressure inside the spinning funnel sucks up water from the surface to join the funnel cloud. Waterspouts do not last very long (up to 20 minutes) and are not as violent as tornadoes. They are common off the coast of Florida and typically have diameters of 12–24 m. Smaller and much less intense funnels of spinning air, invisible until they whirl debris up from the surface, often form over land surfaces that heat up rapidly. They usually last only a few minutes. Unlike tornadoes they are not formed by storm clouds but rise from the ground as warmed, rising air is set spinning by the wind. Small vortices occurring over water are called 'water-devils', those over land 'land-devils'. 'Dust-devils' and 'sand-pillars' occur over dry dusty ground and over desert respectively.

STORM SURGES

Storm surges are exceptionally large waves, often called 'tidal waves' although they are not primarily caused by tides. They are the result of the passage of a fast-moving deep **depression**, and often accompany **hurricanes**. The rapid change of pressure creates a swell wave which grows as it travels across the sea and is channelled onto a coastline. Storm surges cause flooding on low-lying coasts. In Europe, the low lands of the Netherlands and the eastern coasts of the British Isles are particularly at risk, especially when a surge coincides with a high tide. In 1953 a storm surge raised sea level at high-tide by more than 3 m, breaching dykes and sea walls in the Netherlands and in eastern England and causing hundreds of deaths. Storm surges caused by tropical cyclones periodically devastate the low-lying coastal regions of Bangladesh. Very large waves can also be raised by a combination of wind and tide, especially when the wind is blowing uninterrupted across a wide stretch of ocean. 'Tidal' waves due to wind, tide and pressure changes should not be confused with 'tsunami', the large, fast-travelling waves (up to 67 m high) caused by subterranean earthquakes.

🌀 LOCAL WINDS

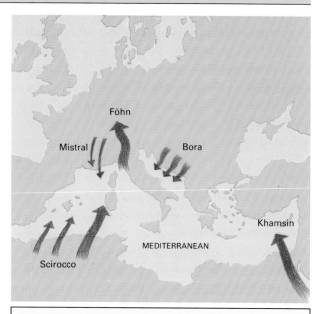

The lie of the land and variations in temperature and pressure generate local and seasonal winds in many parts of the world. In Europe, the dry cold Mistral blows off the Mediterranean coast, especially in Provence. It is caused by cold air north of the Alps being funnelled through the Rhone valley towards a low-pressure area over northeasten Italy (the 'Genoa Low'). Another Mediterranean wind is the Scirocco. This hot south wind blows from the Sahara into the Mediterranean. It picks up moisture as it crosses the Mediterranean and is humid and debilitating by the time it reaches Europe. The infamous warm dry Föhn wind of the Alps is caused by air warming and drying by compression as it flows downhill, and can raise the temperature in the valley by 10–15 °C in an hour. The exceptionally dry air can persist for several days and increases the risk of fire as it drys out wooden buildings and vegetation. Its effects can be psychologically disturbing and it is reported to increase the suicide rate. The Chinook in North America, which blows down from the northeastern Rockies, is a similar wind. Its name means 'snow-eater' as it can clear the slopes of snow in a day.

The sky appears blue because light from the Sun is scattered by the molecules of air and tiny particles in the atmosphere. The shortest wavelengths of light — the blue end of the spectrum — are scattered most. Away from the direct path of the sunlight we therefore see the sky as blue, as we receive the scattered blue rays from all parts of the sky. The shorter the path that sunlight has to travel through the lower atmosphere and the cleaner the atmosphere, the bluer the sky, as only the blue rays are scattered. Direct sunlight is yellow as the longer (red) wavelengths in the beam reach us directly with little scattering. But when the Sun is low in the sky, as at sunset, its rays reach us through a greater thickness of atmosphere. By the time the light reaches our eyes, all the shorter wavelengths have been scattered out of the direct beam, and so the Sun's disc appears much redder and less bright. Scattering of the longer wavelengths also colours the sky red and gold. Polluted skies often look reddish and hazy as the increased number and size of particles in the air scatter the longer wavelengths.

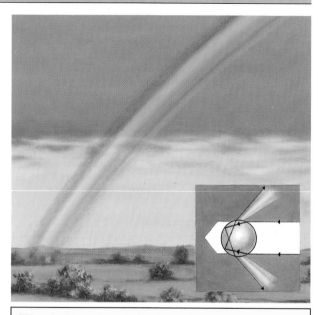

When the Sun comes out after a shower you may see a rainbow as the sunlight is refracted and reflected from millions of raindrops, separating the light rays into the colours of the spectrum. Light bends slightly as it enters a raindrop (refraction) and is then reflected back towards the viewer from the curved back wall of the droplet. So you only see a rainbow when you are standing between the Sun and the curtain of raindrops. Light of different wavelengths is bent at different angles and so the colours become clearly separated, with violet on the inside and red on the outside. Although each droplet refracts the whole spectrum of colours, the viewer sees violet rays from one set of raindrops, yellow from another, and so on, because of the different angles of refraction. The rainbow arc is part of a notional circle with the head of the viewer's shadow as the centre. Each person sees their own unique rainbow and can never reach its end, as the rainbow moves with them as they look at the raindrops from a different angle. Two internal reflections within droplets creates a duller secondary rainbow outside the first, with the order of the colours reversed.

Mountaineers may sometimes see the magnified shadows of themselves or other objects projected onto a bank of cloud or fog below when the Sun is low in the sky behind them. The shadow is enlarged as it falls through a depth of water droplets. Although this strange phenomenon may be seen in any suitable conditions, it is usually called a brockenspectre, after the Brocken, in the Harz mountains of Germany, where it is a familiar sight. The outline of the shadow is surrounded by a 'glory', a many-coloured halo of light, caused by diffraction and reflection of sunlight by the tiny water droplets of the cloud or mist. The viewer can only see the glory around their own shadow, although they can see the shadows of their companions. A glory is also often seen around the shadow of an aircraft projected onto cloud below.

Ice crystals in the atmosphere can produce a range of optical phenomena around the Sun as a result of refraction and reflection of sunlight by the crystals. Sun pillars are vertical beams of light projecting upwards or downwards from the Sun when it is low in the sky, and are caused by reflection of sunlight from the larger ice crystals. Refraction of light through smaller prism-shaped ice crystals creates a variety of effects. The most common are solar and lunar haloes, rings of light surrounding the Sun or Moon when it is veiled by a thin cloud of ice crystals (see **cirrostratus**, page 43 for illustration). The halo is usually white but may be coloured, with the blue colours on the outside of the circle and the red inside. If the ice crystals orient themselves parallel to each other as they fall, the refracted rays combine to produce intense patches of light — parhelia, mock suns or sundogs — which lie on either side of the Sun, on or just outside the radius of the halo. The icy air of the Arctic and Antarctic produces magnificent displays combining haloes, mock suns and sun pillars.

Delicately coloured diffuse rings of light around the Sun or Moon are called coronas. In contrast to haloes, they occur when the Sun or Moon is seen through a thin veil of water droplet cloud or mist. The droplets diffract the sunlight, bending the light rays around the droplet and causing complicated patterns of interference which create the iridescent effect.

MIRAGES

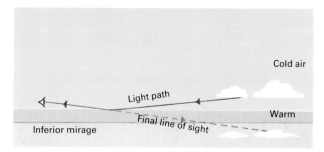

Cold air

Light path

Warm

Final line of sight

Inferior mirage

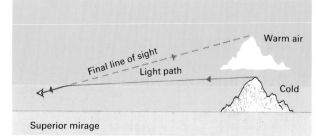

Warm air

Final line of sight

Light path

Cold

Superior mirage

Mirages are the deceptive appearance in the distance of objects that are not really there. They are caused when light coming from a distant object is refracted and reflected at the boundary between layers of cold (dense) and warm (thin) air and thus enters the eye at an unusual angle. The eye is deceived into thinking that the light is actually coming from the point at which it is looking, and so it 'sees' the image there. Inferior mirages occur when there is a thin layer of very hot air at the ground surface. Light from clouds in the sky is reflected off the boundary between the hot air and the colder air above it (upper illustration) and enters the eye at an angle that makes it see the image on the ground far away. The shimmering image, which is often seen in the desert or over a hot road surface, looks like a pool of water in the distance. Superior mirages are formed in cold conditions. Light from a distant object is refracted downwards at the surface of dense cold air near the ground (lower illustration) and so the eye perceives the object up in the sky. Objects below the horizon can become visible, as in the repeat sunsets seen in the Arctic and Antarctic.

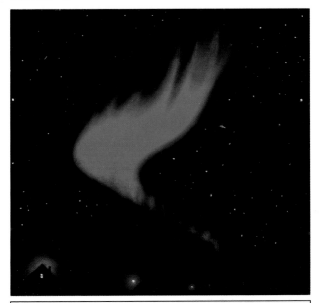

The aurora borealis or Northern Lights are often seen in latitudes higher than 70°, but much less frequently further south. The light is caused by solar discharges of atomic particles that are trapped by the Earth's magnetic field and interact with the upper reaches of the atmosphere to produce radiation. This can take the form of a glow in the sky, shooting rays of light, or waving curtains and ribbons of light. The colours vary from a vivid multi-coloured display to white. A similar spectacle, the aurora australis or Southern Lights is visible in southern polar regions.

Thunderstorms

A severe thunderstorm is one of nature's most striking displays. The sky darkens suddenly, lightning flashes strike the ground amid torrential rain, and thunder bursts out overhead. Thunderstorms are caused by giant **cumulonimbus** clouds. Each cloud is about 5 km across and 5–10 km deep, and individual clouds may last only an hour or so. Transient thunderstorms, sometimes giving no more than a few claps of thunder, are caused by low-based cumulonimbus clouds, which often accompany **cold fronts**, and may occur at any time of year. Longer-lasting thunderstorms usually occur at the end of the summer, when warm air rises into an unstable layer to form high-based thunderclouds. These conditions favour the continual growth of new thunderclouds as the previous ones disperse.

Gathering thunderclouds develop powerful updraughts within them and as the storm approaches, a gentle wind can be felt blowing towards the cloud or there is a short period of calm. As the thundercloud grows to full height a ferocious downdraught develops, bringing heavy rain or hail down from the frozen flattened cloud top (the anvil). The rain rarely lasts long, but can be heavy, and cloudbursts like these can cause local flooding. The downdraught of cold moist air eventually quenches the supply of warm air fuelling the cloud's growth.

Lightning is produced by electrical activity within the cloud. The lightning discharge heats the air in its path; the air glows, and expands and contracts violently, setting up sound waves which we hear as thunder. The distance away of a thunderstorm can be roughly calculated by counting the time in seconds between the lightning flash and the clap of thunder. The light of the flash reaches the observer immediately whereas sound only travels at around $\frac{1}{3}$ km per second. If the thunderstorm is a kilometre away you will hear the thunder 3 seconds after you see the lightning. The rolling thunder that often follows the first sharp thunderclap is caused by echoes from clouds.

Lightning seeks out the shortest path to the ground so that isolated trees or a person out in the open are most at risk of being struck. Tall buildings like church towers and spires used to be particularly vulnerable before the invention of lightning conductors.

Lightning is the result of electrical activity in a thundercloud. Electrical charges separate within the giant cloud. The cloud top becomes positive with most other parts becoming negative. The electrical difference is resolved by powerful electrical discharges that we see as lightning. Discharges can leap from cloud to cloud or from cloud to oppositely charged patches of ground under the cloud. Because air conducts electricity badly, the 'leader stroke' from cloud to ground travels quite slowly, forming a thin branched channel of ionized air which only becomes visible as the leader nears the ground. The blinding flash of forked lightning we see is the 'return stroke' flashing up and down these channels from ground to cloud at high speeds (140,000 km per second) and heating the surrounding air to immensely high temperatures (up to 30,000 °C). Sheet lightning is unseen forked lightning reflected from clouds. There are many anecdotal records of another kind of lightning — ball lightning. This phenomenon, where a ball of glowing light appears and moves around, has no good scientific explanation.

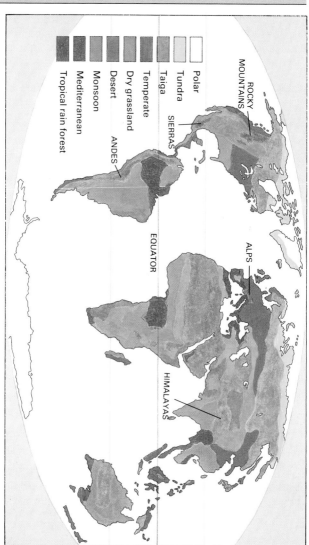

Climate

The climate of an area is an overall description of the type of weather it can expect to have throughout the year. The main determinants of climate are temperature and rainfall and how they vary during the year. The distance from the Equator — the latitude — is one of the main influences on climate. It determines both the average temperature, and whether there are marked differences between seasons. Because the surface of the Earth is curved, the amount of solar radiation received per unit area becomes less as one moves polewards from the Equator. The area around the Equator receives most and the poles least (see **Temperature**). As the Earth is also tilted on its axis the amount of radiation received at the poles, and in the northern and southern mid-latitudes (between 40 and 60°), also varies throughout the year as the Earth makes its annual journey around the Sun. The variation in length of day and night and differences in temperatures at different times of year give clearly marked seasons in these latitudes, each with its own seasonal weather. At the Equator in contrast, day length and temperature is fairly constant throughout the year.

Along the same latitude, climate tends to vary with distance from the sea and whether there are high mountain ranges that create 'rain-shadow' deserts behind them. Maritime regions experience less extreme variation in temperature and rainfall between winter and summer than do continental interiors, as the oceans have a moderating influence. Deep water warms up and cools down much more slowly than land, and so oceans tend to exert a cooling influence in the hottest season and are a source of heat in winter. On a more local scale, a warm ocean **current** nearby can make a region much milder than one might expect for the latitude.

Climatic zones

The combination of rainfall and temperature, and the way they vary throughout the year, give each climatic zone a typical vegetation, and this is how climates are often classified. On the map opposite, the main climate/vegetation zones are marked: glacial (**polar**), **tundra**, cool temperate (**taiga**), warm **temperate**, **mediterranean**, dry grassland (**prairie**, **steppe** and savanna), the monsoon zones where rainfall is highly seasonal, **tropical rain forest**, and **desert**.

The glacial climates of the high Arctic and Antarctic have a mean temperature in the warmest summer month of below 0 °C. There is a permanent cover of snow and ice. The Arctic is an ocean of permanent pack ice surrounded by land, whereas Antarctica is an isolated continent fringed with sea ice and surrounded by ocean. The air is cold and dry, and there is little or no precipitation. What there is falls as snow. The permanent snow cover reflects most of the Sun's radiation, helping to keep temperatures low in summer. Polar conditions also occur on the tops of high mountains outside the polar regions. At the poles themselves there is a period of around 6 months continuous daylight in 'summer' and 6 months of continuous night in 'winter'. The harshest conditions on Earth are those of the Antarctic plateau, where the polar cold is intensified by altitude above sea level and strong winds. At the Soviet base of Vostok, over 3000 metres above sea level, mean annual temperature is −57 °C and average temperature in July (the Antarctic winter) can be as low as −88 °C. Snowfall has never been recorded.

In the Arctic, the lands immediately around the permanent polar ice sheet form the tundra, a vast treeless region extending to the northern limit at which plants can grow. The mean temperature in the warmest month in summer rises above 0 °C but never exceeds 10 °C. This is enough, however, to melt the snow and allow plants to grow. A metre below the surface the ground remains permanently frozen. The vegetation of lichens, moss and grass, perennial flowers and a few dwarf shrubs is adapted to make the most of the short summer, which may only last a month or two. In the winter, the persistent snow cover helps to insulate the surface vegetation from the low temperatures (down to −30 °C for January). Although precipitation is low (usually less than 250 mm per year) the ground is moist as the melted snow cannot drain through the frozen layer and does not evaporate in the cool air. A similar type of vegetation is found further south on high mountains. In the Alps, a 'tundra' zone starts at around 2000 metres.

To the south of the tundra lies the taiga, a zone of mainly coniferous forest mixed with hardy deciduous trees like birches and willows. It is defined by mean temperature in the warmest summer month (July) above 10 °C and a mean temperature in the coldest winter month of below −3 °C. It extends throughout central Scandinavia, the USSR and Canada. Long cold dry winters are followed by a short summer. Almost all rain and snow fall between May and October and some of the greatest extremes in the world between winter and summer temperatures are experienced in the continental interiors. A range from 30 °C in July to −30 °C in January is quite usual.

Most of Europe has a temperate climate, characterized by a mean temperature in the hottest month of more than 10 °C and rain (or snow in winter) all the year round. Paris and London, for example, are driest in spring (around 42 mm rainfall in April) and wettest in autumn and winter (56 mm in January (Paris) and 58 mm in October (London)). Within this broad climatic type the mild and changeable maritime climates of western Europe and northwestern North America contrast with the continental climates of central Europe, eastern North America and northeastern Asia. Rainfall ranges from 50 to more than 350 cm per year (in the Pacific northwest). In maritime areas temperatures rarely rise above 25 °C or fall for long below 0 °C. Continental areas are hotter in summer, with rainfall in the form of thundery showers, and colder and drier in winter, when sub-zero temperatures persist for long periods. The natural vegetation cover for temperate Europe and eastern North America is broad-leaved deciduous forest, now largely cleared for agriculture; on the northwest coast of North America it is coniferous forest, in which grow the largest trees in the world.

Around the Mediterranean sea the climate is hot and dry in summer and mild and moist in winter, with mean summer temperatures between 20 and 27°C and winter temperatures between 4 and 13°C. Rainfall is between 10 and 80 cm and falls mostly in winter, between November and March. It rarely snows but night frosts can occur in winter. This type of climate is also found in California, parts of Chile, South Africa and southwestern Australia. Evergreen trees such as (in Europe) the holm oak and cork oak, and conifers, especially pines, are the natural cover, but centuries of overgrazing and clearance around the Mediterranean have mostly replaced this open forest with maquis (low scrub and thickets of small evergreen trees). The Mediterranean is subject to several distinctive **local winds**. As well as the Mistral and the Scirocco, the cold north-easterly Bora blows from the interior of former Yugoslavia to the lower coastlands, the cool dry northerly Tramontana blows across the Spanish Mediterranean coast, and the moist Levanter blows from the eastern Mediterranean to the straits of Gibraltar.

The original dry grassland of the North American prairie has now been transformed into one of the main wheat-growing areas of the world. The grasslands of the northern hemisphere — steppes and prairies — occur in the interiors of North America and Eurasia, cut off from moisture-laden winds by the mountain barrier of the Rocky Mountains on the one hand, and distance from the ocean on the other. Long severe winters with sub-zero temperatures and snow follow short, warm summers with temperatures between 16 and 20 °C. With precipitation (snow and rain) of less than 100 cm per year it is generally too dry for trees to grow well and continuous forest to develop. The natural vegetation is grass and grassland flowers. Other temperate grasslands are the veldt of South Africa, the pampas of South America and the downs of Australia. Tropical grasslands include the savannas of Africa, between the equatorial rain forest and the Sahara. At the desert margins annual rainfall is low (around 25–50 cm) and highly seasonal, and summer temperatures reach 40 °C. Rainfall is 90–150 cm per year nearer the Equator, but as water evaporates in the high temperatures the land is still dry.

On either side of the Equator, between latitudes around 5 °S and 10 °N, rainfall of between 200 and 400 cm and constant temperatures of around 27 °C support the luxuriant tropical rain forest. There are no marked seasons so near the Equator and growth continues throughout the year. The high rainfall comes from the **cumulus** clouds that form continually in the warm air rising at the Equator (see **General Circulation**) and **thunderstorms** are common. The main areas of tropical rain forest are in the Amazon basin of South America, the basin of the Zaire in Africa, and in southeast Asia, extending from Sri Lanka to Thailand and through the Philippines and Malaysia to Papua-New Guinea and the extreme northwest of Australia. Tropical rain forest is now disappearing at an alarming rate.

Deserts lie under areas of almost permanent atmospheric high pressure or are shielded from moist winds by high mountain barriers. Rainfall is less than 10 cm per annum and erratic, and evaporates rapidly. The Atacama desert on the west coast of South America has less than 2 cm of rain per year. This coastal strip is desert because prevailing winds blow not from the sea but from the interior, and are blocked by the Andes. Some places in the Atacama have had almost no rain for hundreds of years. Temperatures in hot deserts soar to over 40°C in daytime in summer but desert nights can be cold as the bare ground loses heat rapidly. Desert plants are adapted to conserve moisture and are succulents like cacti, spiny shrubs, or annuals which lie dormant as seeds until the rain comes. The largest desert in the world is the Sahara, with its shifting dunes of sand and the highest recorded temperature of 57.8°C. The other main hot deserts are the central Australian desert, the Atacama, and the Kalahari in Southern Africa. The Gobi desert of central Asia and the North American desert of California and Arizona are sometimes termed 'cold' deserts because of their low winter temperatures.

Weather Observation

Although we grumble at the weather forecast when we get caught in an unexpected downpour, short-term weather forecasts are nowadays probably as accurate as they can be. Local variations occur within the space of even a few miles, and if you get to know the tricks of your local weather you can often interpret the general weather forecast better.

The forecasts put out by national Meteorological Offices depend on gathering as much information about weather and atmospheric conditions from as many places as possible. At set times of the day, data from individual weather stations are relayed to regional and national forecasting centres. The information is then fed into computers and rapidly plotted onto charts to give a snapshot picture of atmospheric conditions over the whole area at a particular point in time. As weather does not keep to national boundaries, weather centres worldwide are linked into an international network and exchange information. Once all the data have been processed, experienced meteorologists draw in isobars and **fronts** and make a forecast of the weather for a particular area for periods from a few hours to a few days ahead. Nowadays, they are aided by some of the most powerful computers in the world, and by satellite pictures that show weather systems approaching.

Daily national and regional forecasts are released to the general public through the press, television and radio, and more localized and specialized forecasts are prepared for those whose livelihood, or even their life, depends on the weather.

The raw data on which forecasts are based come from ground-based weather stations and ships, from weather balloons carrying instruments high into the troposphere, and from satellites looking down on the Earth from space.

But you don't need a satellite to make a study of the weather yourself. You can keep a useful weather diary with just a few items of equipment. A **barometer** to measure atmospheric pressure and a maximum and minimum **thermometer** to measure temperature are essentials. A simple **rain gauge** to measure rainfall is easily constructed and use the Beaufort Scale (see pages 124/125) to estimate wind speed. Learn to recognize the types of clouds in the sky and to measure the amount of cloud cover by eye.

PRESSURE

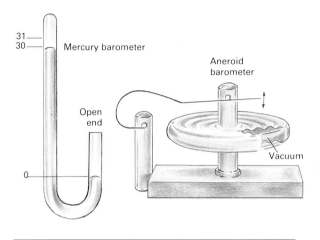

Mercury barometer

Aneroid barometer

Open end

Vacuum

mb	965	982	999	1016	1033
in	28.5	29.0	29.5	30.0	30.5
mm	724	737	749	762	775

Atmospheric pressure is measured by a barometer. There are two main types — mercury and aneroid. The mercury barometer measures atmospheric pressure by the height of the column of mercury it supports. The aneroid type has an internal sealed compartment partially emptied of air with a thin corrugated lid that moves in and out as pressure changes. It is slightly less accurate than a mercury barometer but more convenient. Ignore the markings 'Rain', 'Change' and 'Fair' which traditionally ornament the dials of household barometers. Although high pressure often goes with fine weather and low pressure with bad, this is not always so, and it is the changes in pressure, rather than the absolute pressures, that will help you to forecast the weather. Unless you are at sea level, you will need to calibrate the barometer for the change in pressure with altitude, so that you can compare your readings with those given by the weather service. Your local weather centre will help. Modern barometers are marked in millibars (running from around 950–1050 mb); older instruments will have the equivalent in inches (28–31) or mm (700–787) of mercury.

TEMPERATURE & HUMIDITY

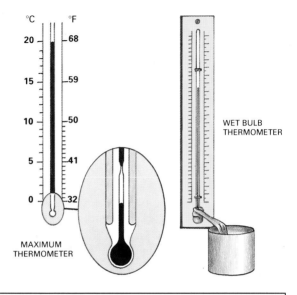

°C °F

20 — 68

15 — 59

10 — 50

5 — 41

0 — 32

MAXIMUM
THERMOMETER

WET BULB
THERMOMETER

Air temperature is measured in degrees Celsius (°C) or degrees Fahrenheit (°F)★, by a thermometer placed in a shaded, well ventilated position outside. To shield thermometers from the heating effect of direct sunlight they are usually placed behind a 'Stevenson screen', the white slatted box you see at a weather station. A north-facing wall is the best alternative for the casual observer. An inexpensive thermometer for use in equable climates is a maximum/minimum garden thermometer with which you can record the maximum daytime and minimum night-time temperatures. In official weather recordings an alcohol thermometer is used to measure minimum temperatures as mercury freezes at −39.87 °C. A mercury thermometer with the bulb covered in muslin kept damp from a water reservoir becomes a 'wet-bulb' thermometer for measuring **humidity**. In dry air, water evaporates rapidly from the muslin, cooling the thermometer; in saturated air, evaporation is non-existent and the thermometer registers the ambient air temperature. The difference in the readings from a 'wet-bulb' and an ordinary thermometer gives a measure of the humidity.

★ Conversion of °F to °C. °C = $\frac{5}{9}$ (°F − 32); °F = (°C × $\frac{9}{5}$) + 32.

As well as the barometer (usually placed indoors) and a range of thermometers housed in their Stevenson screen, a basic weather station will also include a rain gauge (1) for measuring rainfall. This is a metal container with a standard sized funnel opening which is placed away from obstacles and emptied at set periods. The water is measured, and converted into millimetres (or inches) of rainfall — that is, the depth to which the rain (or snow) falling in a certain period would cover the ground if it did not drain away or evaporate. A home-made rain gauge is easily improvised. Cloud cover costs nothing to measure as it is assessed by eye in eighths of total sky area covered (oktas). Clear sky is reported as 0/8; completely overcast, 8/8; and half clouded, 4/8; or by symbols as depicted in the Glossary. The sky in the picture is half clouded. Scattered clouds are brought together into one mass for measurement purposes. The traditional saying that if you can see a patch of blue sky 'big enough to make a Dutchman a pair of trousers' the cloud will soon disperse, is true enough for the thin layer of early morning cloud that forms in moist warm air in spring and summer.

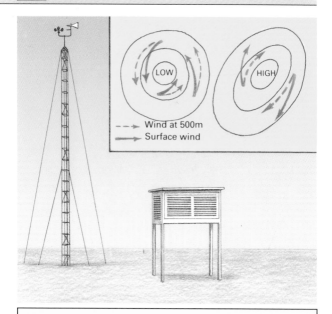

Wind at 500m
Surface wind

An official weather station will be equipped with instruments like the cup anemometer for measuring wind speed, which is generally reported as the average speed over a 10 minute period. The anemometer is mounted on a mast together with a wind vane to show direction. A useful estimate of wind speed can be made by the amateur using the Beaufort Scale (pages 124/125). Estimating wind direction is often difficult, especially in the average urban back garden surrounded by buildings and trees. Looking at the direction in which the clouds are moving can help, but remember that, compared with the direction of clouds at around 500 m high, wind near the ground is deflected by friction by as much as 20 or 30° towards a centre of low pressure or outward from a high pressure centre. Use the Buys Ballot Law (page 83) to determine where the area of low pressure is.

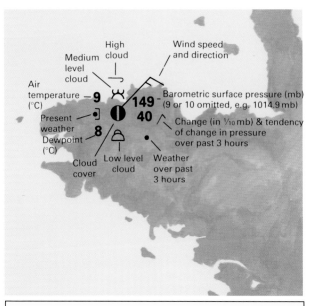

After noting temperature, pressure and direction of change, wind direction and speed, cloud cover and cloud types, you should complete the diary by recording the actual weather for the day. Meteorologists officially distinguish a hundred or so different types of weather and weather phenomena you may encounter, from drizzle to a tornado. But you can record the weather clearly in terms of a few commonsense categories: (1) state of the sky (is it blue, partly cloudy, cloudy or overcast?); (2) precipitation (is it raining, drizzling, showery, snowing, hailing, or sleeting? and if so is it light, heavy, continuous or intermittent?); (3) electrical phenomena (are you in the middle of a thunderstorm, or can you hear distant thunder and see distant lightning?); (4) visibility (is it misty, hazy, foggy); and (5) ground phenomena (dew, hoar frost). The illustration shows how the state of the weather and atmospheric conditions at a point in time are summarized on weather station records using internationally agreed symbols (see Glossary).

BALLOONS & SATELLITES

Observations at ground-level can only give part of the weather picture. To make accurate forecasts meteorologists also need to know what atmospheric conditions are like higher up. Weather balloons carry instruments up to altitudes of 35 km to measure temperature, pressure and humidity. The information is relayed continuously to the ground by radio signals. Our knowledge of world weather has also been transformed by satellites. Geostationary satellites, some 36,000 km above the Equator, move over it at the same speed as the Earth's rotation and so view the same area all the time. Polar orbiting satellites circle the Earth from pole to pole at around 840 km high, taking 100 minutes to complete an orbit. They observe a band of the Earth's surface around 3000 km wide at each orbit and cover the whole of the globe in 24 hours as it rotates beneath them, relaying a continuous picture which is picked up in turn by receiving stations around the globe. Satellites give a bird's-eye view of weather systems and are especially valuable to scan the oceans, the poles and the tropics where surface measurements are scarce.

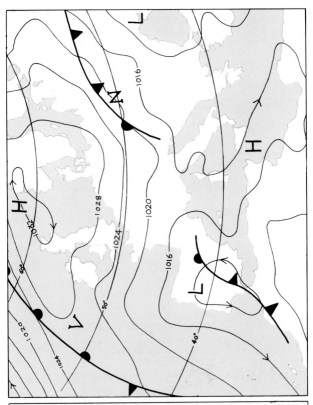

Weather charts like these are prepared each day by National Meteorological Services from many sets of station recordings like those depicted on page 117. Surface pressure is mapped, isobars drawn, and the positions of fronts estimated. This chart shows the situation on a summer's day. A warm front (V) is situated in the Atlantic and is prevented from moving eastwards by the large area of high pressure (H) over the northern British Isles and Scandinavia.

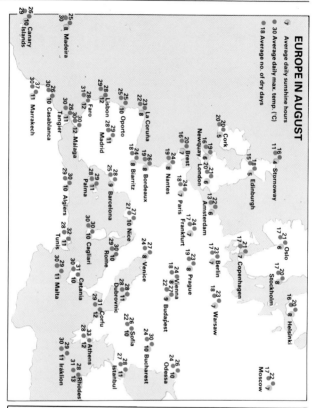

EUROPE IN AUGUST

- Average daily sunshine hours
- Average daily max. temp. (°C)
- Average no. of dry days

To help you plan your holiday, Meteorological Services provide information on the conditions you can expect in the main cities and holiday areas throughout the year. This map shows average temperatures, number of hours of sunshine daily and number of dry days throughout Europe during August.

SHIPPING FORECAST

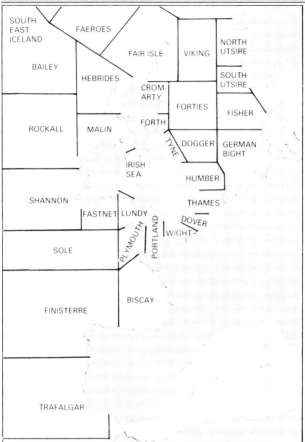

Ships at sea receive special weather bulletins. The seas around the British Isles and western Europe are divided into defined areas. Official meteorological services provide information on present and forecast conditions which is transmitted to shipping by fax, telephone and regular radio broadcasts. Gale warnings are issued when winds of Force 8 or greater, or gusts of 43 to 51 knots are expected.

Index

Acid rain	72
Air masses	28, 29
Altocumulus	44
Altostratus	45
Anticyclones	32
Atmosphere	14, 15
Aurora	99
Avalanche	81
Banner cloud	59
Barometer	113
Blizzards	80
Breezes	86
Brockenspectre	95
Castellanus clouds	56
Cirrocumulus	42
Cirrostratus	43
Cirrus	41
Climate	102, 103
Desert	111
Mediterranean	108
Polar	104
Prairie	109
Taiga	106
Temperate	107
Tropical rain forest	110
Tundra	105
Steppe	109
Cloud (see also individual types)	37
Cloud caps	57
Cloud cover	38, 115
Cloud formation	39
Cloud streets	51
Cloud types	40
Cold front	34
Contrails	60
Coriolis effect	83
Corona	97
Cumulonimbus	54
Cumulus	50
Cumulus congestus	52
Currents	23
Cyclones	31
Depressions	31
Dew	66
Distrails	60
Drizzle	73
Drought	76
Dust-devils	90
Floods	75
Fog	61
Föhn wind	92
Forecasting	112
Fronts	30, 33–35
Frost	67
Gales	87
General Circulation	20, 21
Global winds	84, 85
Glory	95
Greenhouse effect	17, 18
Hail	77
Haloes	43, 96
Holiday weather	120
Humidity	24, 114
Hurricane	88
Ice crystals	79
Jet streams	21
Land-devils	90
Lenticular clouds	58
Lightning	101
Local winds	92
Mamma	55
Mirages	98
Mist	61
Mistral	92
Mock suns	96
Monsoon	23
Mountain clouds	57–59
Nimbostratus	46
Occluded front	35
Ozone layer	14, 16
Parhelia	96
Pileus	53
Pressure	19, 113
Radiation fog	62
Rain	69, 70, 71

Rainbow 94
Rainfall 115
Red sky at night 36

Sand-pillars 90
Satellites 118
Scirocco 92
Scud 49
Sea fog 63
Showers 74
Sky colour 93
Smog 65
Snow 78
Snowflakes 79
Steam fog 64
Storm surges 91
Storms 87
Stratocumulus 47
Stratus 48
Sun dogs 96
Sun pillar 96

Temperature 17, 18, 20, 114
Thunderstorms 100
Tornado 89
Tower clouds 56

Virga 73

Warm Front 33
Warm rain 71
Water 24, 25, 69
Water cycle 25, 68, 69
Water-devils 90
Waterspout 90
Weather balloons 118
Weather maps 27, 119, 120, 121
Weather observation 112
Weather recording 117
Weather systems 26
Wind 20, 21, 82, 116

The Beaufort Scale

Force	Description	Sea state	Effects on land	Speed (knots)
0	Calm	Sea like mirror	No wind: smoke rises vertically	<1
1	Light air	Ripples with appearance of scales, no foam crests	No noticeable wind; vanes remain still but smoke drifts	1–3
2	Light breeze	Wavelets, small but pronounced. Glassy crests do not break.	Wind felt on face; vanes move, leaves rustle	4–6
3	Gentle breeze	Large wavelets, crests begin to break. Glassy foam, occasional white horses	Hair, clothing disturbed; light flag extended, leaves and small twigs move constantly	7–10
4	Moderate breeze	Small waves becoming longer, frequent white horses	Hair disarranged; raises dust and loose paper, moves small branches	11–16
5	Fresh breeze	Moderate waves of long form. Many white horses, some spray	Disagreeable wind, force felt on body; small trees in leaf begin to sway	17–21
6	Strong breeze	Some large waves, extensive white foam crests, some spray	Difficult to walk steadily; umbrellas hard to control; large branches move; telegraph wires whistle	22–27